Ne

Muriel Dreifuss, Max Block
and Anne Samachson

CITYSCAPE

JPMGUIDES

New York consists of five boroughs—Brooklyn, the Bronx, Queens, Staten Island and Manhattan. But for millions of visitors, New York is the island of Manhattan. The heart of the city, 21 km (13 miles) long and 3 km (2 miles) wide, Manhattan encompasses just about everything you'll want to see and experience in the Big Apple.

Contents

Symbols

★ Our favourites
🅢 Subway station

cityLights

The World's City

Whether you approach it by sea, land or air, New York is one of those rare cities that can inspire love at first sight. There comes a particular moment when that stunning Manhattan skyline suddenly comes into view, when its familiar image converges abruptly with the stark reality of its glittering buildings. Pause on the threshold of one of the greatest cities on earth, a city that is at once exhilarating, overwhelming, bewildering and mysterious. Within minutes, you find yourself hurtling through a tunnel or over a bridge—any of the many concrete and steel arteries that pump its lifeblood into the island-city—until you stand, awestruck, in the midst of this amazing creation.

All its museums, cafés and monuments notwithstanding, Manhattan is, first and foremost, testament to mankind's curious habit of living in close proximity to other humans. You are surrounded by the mad procession of cars, the cacophony of horns, the blur of city lights and hectic throngs of people. It won't take long to realise that, while you've come to see a thriving American city, what will greet you is the world. Welcome to the Big Apple!

The constant influx of energy, creativity and ingenuity from other shores has set this city apart. New York is home to some 2 million foreigners: one in every four people living in Manhattan, the Bronx, Queens, Staten Island or Brooklyn was born in another country. More than 120 languages are spoken here, including Hindi, Arabic, Hebrew, Punjabi and Thai, and some 50 major religions are practised in 3,500 places of worship. Every year, dozens of parades celebrate the cultural heritages of various immigrant communities. The physical structure of New York, as well, is a blend of immigrant flavours: John Roebling, a German immigrant, engineered the Brooklyn Bridge, I.M. Pei, an immigrant from China, designed the Jacob Javits Convention Center, Hungarian-born Marcel Breuer was the architect of the Whitney Museum and Andrew Carnegie, a former Scot, established Carnegie Hall. Even one of the great symbols of the city, the Statue of Liberty, is herself an immigrant from France.

There is no question that the constant inflow of newcomers is what allows New York its penchant for re-invention, its uncanny ability to transform itself overnight, to maintain its vitality, its colour, its excitement and its warmth.

What First?

New York City is home to dozens of museums, thousands of restaurants, hundreds of theatres and one of the busiest harbours in the world. There is so much to see and do that the most difficult problem you will have to face is deciding where to go first. It's a good idea to get right down to business and take in the stunning panoramic view from the observation deck of the Empire State Building or the top of Rockefeller Center. Alternatively, you can catch a boat around the island and imprint the Manhattan skyline on your memory.

Eager to start shopping? The city is packed with treasures for every taste and every budget. Prefer a Broadway show? You'll find discount tickets on sale downtown and in Times

Square. If you're feeling adventurous, you can try some experimental theatre outside the theatre district. Music? For starters, you can listen to some great jazz, fantastic blues, innovative rock, romantic cabaret or breathtaking opera. Of course, you shouldn't forget to visit a museum. There's a bounty of them on Fifth Avenue; indeed, the stretch between 70th and 104th streets is called "Museum Mile". Art-lovers will be pleased to know that the Metropolitan Museum of Art, Cooper-Hewitt, Guggenheim, Whitney, Neue Galerie and Museum of Modern Art are all within easy walking distance of one another.

Maybe you would like to do something out of the ordinary, like playing chess in one of the oldest parks in the city. Jump into the next cab, head over to Washington Square and join a game in the southwest corner. West of the park, on the corner of Sixth Avenue and 4th St, you can watch some of the best street basketball in the city.

By now you'll be thinking it's time to eat. The food! Afghan, African, Argentinean, Brazilian, Burmese, Cambodian, Chilean, Chinese, Cuban, Ethiopian, Greek, Indian, Jamaican, Lebanese, Malaysian, Mexican, Moroccan, Peruvian, Pakistani, Polish, Russian, Sri Lankan—around the world in a culinary bonanza! You'll have your pick of everything from elegant French cuisine to deli sandwiches bursting at the seams, juicy burgers and smokey barbecued ribs. You don't eat meat? Some of the most innovative eateries are strictly vegetarian.

Rubbing Shoulders with the World

Regardless of what you do in New York, you're bound to have a good time. And wherever you go, you'll be rubbing shoulders with people from all over the world, hearing them speak different languages, tasting their foods, looking at their beautiful faces. New York is bound to leave you with the unmistakable impression that you've witnessed a bit of every country on earth. And, in more senses than one, you have.

cityPast

As you make your way past the shops on Fifth Avenue and the outdoor cafés in Greenwich Village, consider this: the ground you are walking on was once dense forest. Thick shrubs and berry plants, creeks and ponds dotted the island. Deer, raccoons, wolves and foxes foraged inland, while turtles, salamanders, toads and frogs thrived near the marshes and swamps. Oysters were abundant in the shallows surrounding the island; dozens of species of birds lived in the overhead canopy of trees. And throughout, in small communities of grass long-houses surrounded by farmland, Native tribes traded, cultivated crops, celebrated religious festivals, raised families and fashioned intricate tools. It was, indeed, a natural paradise.

Discovery

The Lenape, later named the Delaware by Europeans, greeted the Italian explorer Giovanni da Verrazano when he landed in 1524 at what is now Staten Island. Verrazano stirred up appreciable interest upon his return to France, but colonization of the New World would have to wait. The treacherous voyage across the Atlantic, the danger of battles with the natives and diplomatic tangles between the European powers prevented any serious conquest of North America for the next century.

In 1609, the Englishman Henry Hudson sailed into what is now New York Harbor. He had been sent by the Dutch, in hopes of discovering a westerly route to India. Impressed with the furs, fruit and tobacco that Hudson brought back, the Dutch West India Company secured a charter to set up a colony and, in 1624, thirty Protestant families arrived to establish the settlement of New Amsterdam at the southern tip of Manhattan Island. In 1626, the Lenape sold the island to Peter Minuit, the first governor of the colony, for the now famously insignificant sum of $24 worth of goods.

Setting Down Roots

Constant battles with the natives, and a young government that couldn't decide if it was running a business or a colony, were obstacles that the Dutch settlers struggled to overcome. In 1664, the British elbowed their way into New Amsterdam—with little resistance on the part of the Dutch—and New York was born. And the Lenape? By the time the British arrived, the 2,000-year-old native society had been virtually obliterated by smallpox, malaria, alcohol and the unsettling habit of the Dutch to periodically slaughter their new neighbours.

The British had a much better time of it than the Dutch. Under their supervision, New York became a powerful centre of trade, supplying Europe with furs, tobacco, sugar and tea. The foundations of a proper city were established during the hundred-year period of British control: libraries and theatres were opened, King's College—the precursor to Columbia University—was founded, a municipal government with a mayor was installed, the first daily newspaper was published, and streets, houses, businesses and public buildings stretched further north. By 1770, the population had grown to 20,000, consisting primarily of the British, the remnants of the Dutch community and roughly 1,500 African slaves. Treatment of the slaves was harsh. Usually forced to work as domestic servants, they were barred from owning property, prevented from socializing in groups of more than three and forced to obey a curfew. If even a rumour of rebellion reached British ears, the slaves were often brutally punished or even executed.

Unrest

In an effort to subsidize their vast empire, the British parliament levied heavy taxes on the colonies in the New World. By 1775, the colonists had grown tired of sending their hard-earned money back to Great Britain. The struggle for independence began. There was a considerable effort on the part of the colonial Patriots to expel the British from New York throughout the war, but the Royal Navy had surrounded Manhattan Island. During the American Revolution, New York remained under British control.

His Majesty's troops surrendered in 1781, and the British began to leave New York two years later. But the colonists found their home in complete disarray at the close of the war. Much of the city had been destroyed during the fighting, there was little revenue as most trade had been suspended, and the sudden return to New York of thousands of Patriot soldiers presented serious problems. A housing shortage, poverty, disease and general discontent seized the city as it entered the 19th century.

Rebuilding

James Duane, the first mayor after the war, helped lift New York out of this dire situation. Docks and wharves were built along the East River to provide better anchorage for ships and encourage trading along the Atlantic coast. Streets were improved and sewers installed. A banking centre in the Wall Street area was constructed, together with a new City Hall. By 1800 New York had re-established itself as a strong hub of trade and commerce.

The completion in 1825 of the Erie Canal—a waterway connecting the Hudson River and the Great Lakes—bolstered New York's status as a major seaport and manufacturing centre. Goods were now more easily sold and transported to the west, and whatever New York City could not produce itself (coal, for instance) was shipped in via the canal. Sugar, flour, liquor and clothing were major exports during this period, spurring manufacturing and creating jobs. Expansion took hold of the city like a hurricane. Many of the original Dutch houses were torn down to make room for shops and banks, streets were lengthened and widened, and opulent private residences sprang up. Central Park was built, St Patrick's Cathedral completed, and wealthy families like the Rocke-

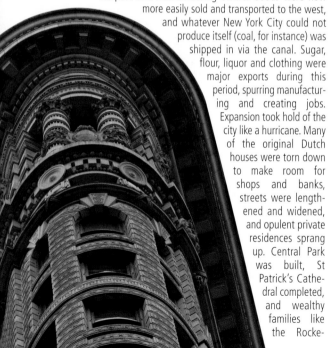

fellers, the Vanderbilts, the Fricks and the Carnegies assured themselves a place in New York's aristocracy by amassing huge fortunes, building palatial mansions along Fifth Avenue and creating a number of educational and cultural institutions.

A Working Community

The commercial growth of New York City in the first half of the 19th century, massive though it was, paled in comparison to the enormous population growth. From 1820 to 1860, the numbers soared from 123,000 to 813,000, an explosion that was due in large part to the poor economic conditions in Europe. Irish and Germans, in particular, flooded the city. About half of these immigrants were able to find jobs as servants, garment workers, cooks, and manual labourers. Others worked as skilled craftsmen, and some eventually opened up their own businesses as tailors, jewellers and bakers.

Immigrant neighbourhoods consisting primarily of Italians or Germans, Scandinavians or Russians, Jews or Irish, began popping up. Cramped living conditions, lack of clean water, light and air, poor sanitation, disease and crime were constant problems. While the horrific conditions were ignored by most of the city, newcomers like Lillian Wald, who founded the Henry Street Settlement House, and immigrants like Danish-born Jacob Riis, who exposed the suffering in the slums, convinced authorities to replace the orphanages and poorhouses with schools and social services.

At the same time, the immigrants began to form labour unions. Allegiances that transcended nationality were established with the hope of improving the lives of all immigrant labourers: Irish and Germans formed the Central Labor Union in 1882 to press for better wages. A group of Jewish and Italian women founded the International Ladies Garment Union in order to secure a 52-hour working week, overtime pay and legal holidays. Sydney Hillman, a Russian-born Jew, led the Amalgamated Clothing Workers of America in their fight for unemployment insurance, affordable cooperative housing and the creation of banks to fit the needs of the working class.

Expansion and Restriction

As conditions and wages improved, so too did productivity. In 1870, the first railcar was introduced, carrying 400,000 passengers in its first year of operation. In 1877, the American Museum of Natural History was opened, followed shortly by the Metropolitan Museum of Art and the Metropolitan Opera House. The Statue of Liberty was unveiled in 1886, the New York Public Library opened in 1895 and, in 1898, the city of Greater New York was established, encompassing Manhattan, Brooklyn, Queens, the Bronx and Staten Island.

New York continued to grow at the dawn of the 20th century. Between 1892 and 1954, 12 million people passed through the Port of New York at Ellis Island; today, nearly half of all Americans have at least one ancestor who did so. There, just off the coast of Manhattan, immigrants were registered, examined, and, if accepted, sent by ferry to lower Manhattan. Many continued further into the interior of the United States or along the eastern seaboard before settling down, but a third of these immigrants remained in New York.

These new immigrants were accused of spreading poverty, filth and disease, of stealing jobs and committing crimes. The federal government responded by passing a series of laws to regulate the number of foreigners entering the country. The Chinese and Japanese were barred from entering the US, and criminals, contract labourers or anyone thought to be suffering from insanity or contagious disease were also excluded.

Great Depression and Aftermath

By 1920, the population of New York and its boroughs had risen to about 5.5 million. Remarkably, 40 per cent of the city's residents were foreign-born. In October 1929, the stock market crashed, closing businesses throughout the city and leaving thousands of Americans unemployed. Mayor Fiorello La Guardia, the son of an Italian immigrant father, implemented plans for the construction of bridges and tunnels, schools, parks, hospitals and highways, creating jobs for New Yorkers and transforming the infrastructure of the city. Massive construction wasn't limited to government projects; two of the city's best known skyscrapers, the Chrysler Building and the Empire State Building, opened during the Great Depression, which lasted until World War II.

After the war, New York maintained its reputation as one of the most important commercial centres in the world. But during the postwar period,

Manhattan renewed its reputation as a cultural and artistic hot spot. It was said that in 1960, more than two-thirds of the country's better-known artists were living in New York, including Jackson Pollock, Mark Rothko, Robert Rauschenberg and Andy Warhol.

Today, the city continues to attract people from throughout the world. The latest waves of immigrants include Koreans, Africans, Central Americans, Indians, Mexicans and West Indians. New York's ethnic communities are thriving, doubling as welcoming committees for the new arrivals and helping to shape New York in ways that are invaluable and irreplaceable.

THE CANYON OF HEROES

All of New York's ticker-tape parades have taken place on Lower Broadway in the Financial District. Held to honour distinguished visitors and triumphal occasions, they led to this area being called the Canyon of Heroes. The first ticker-tape parade occurred spontaneously in 1886, when excited brokerage workers threw ribbons of paper tape (used to print stock quotes) out of windows during the dedication of the Statue of Liberty. Soon, flurries of paper swirling through the air were seen as the ultimate symbol of the city's approval.

Every parade (about 200 to date) is commemorated by a strip of granite embedded in the sidewalk of Lower Broadway.

Look down as you stroll along, and you'll see a roster of all those who have received New York's greatest accolade. Among them are Edward, Prince of Wales (1919), Charles Lindbergh (1927), Winston Churchill (1946), Ben Hogan (1953), Elizabeth II (1957), Charles de Gaulle (1960), Pope John Paul II (1979) and the New York Yankees (2000).

OCTOBER 23, 1998 ★ NEW YORK YANKEES, WORLD SERIES CHAMPIONS

LIFE UNDERGROUND

More than just a means of transportation, New York's century-old subway system shapes the city's art, culture and commerce. The trains have inspired films (*The Taking of Pelham 1, 2, 3*), songs (Duke Ellington's *Take the A Train*) and books (*Subwayland* by Randy Kennedy).

The system has its own museum located in an old subway station in Brooklyn Heights. At the **New York Transit Museum** you can explore 19 lovingly restored subway cars and other exhibits (Boerum Place and Schermerhorn St ☎ 1 718-694-3451). The Museum's annex store in Grand Central Terminal shows changing exhibitions, too. Visit either location to stock up on unique subway-themed souvenirs.

Thanks to the MTA's famed **Arts for Transit** programme, original artworks are installed in many stations. The pieces are often inspired by places and events connected to their locations. Outstanding installations include the whimsical bronze figurines of Tom Otterness' *Life*

Underground (14th St/8th Ave station), and the mosaics of Jane Dickson's *The Revelers*, depicting New Year's Eve celebrants (Times Square station), the Museum of Natural History's *For Want of A Nail*, showing the evolution of life (81st St station), Faith Ringgold's *Flying Home Harlem Heroes and Heroines* (125th St station), and Deborah Brown's *Platform Diving* (Houston St station).

Susan Cagle in her busking days.

The MTA's **Music Under New York** project brings live, quality music and performance underground. More than 100 soloists and groups participate, performing in prime locations and displaying the official banner. The roster includes classical violinists, soul singers, jazz ensembles, bluesmen, jugglers, tap dancers, steel drummers, opera and folk singers. Some who start here go on to bigger and better things. Susan Cagle, a performer discovered in a subway station, has been signed by a major music label and is appearing in independent films.

citySights

FINANCIAL DISTRICT

Skyscraper National Park: that's novelist Kurt Vonnegut's apt term for New York. Whereas other cities grew outwards, New York grew up. And up, and up. While there are plenty of beautiful landmarks that don't shoot a thousand feet into the air, the skyscrapers are the true architectural wonders in New York.

THE DISTRICT AT A GLANCE

City Hall (B7) The city government headquarters took nine years to complete, from 1803. A yellow fever epidemic was blamed for the delay, but a wages dispute contributed, too. In Federal style (inspired by English neoclassicism), the building is understated, elegant and finely detailed. Tours are free but call ahead; reservations are required. The domed rotunda in the lobby, the Governor's Room and the Blue Room, where the mayor holds press conferences, are big draws.

☎ 1 212 788-2170 or 311 from within the City • Broadway and Murray St
Ⓢ 4, 5, 6: Brooklyn Bridge/City Hall; R, W: City Hall; 2, 3: Park Place

Yellow cabs—a fast way across Manhattan, till you get stuck in a traffic jam.

Woolworth Building (B7) By 1913, F.W. Woolworth, a retail pioneer and founder of a chain of discount stores that priced merchandise at 5 and 10 cents, had amassed a fortune big enough to pay $13,500,000 cash for the construction of this building, at the time the tallest in the world at 241 m (792 ft). It was nicknamed "the Cathedral of Commerce" for its resemblance to European Gothic cathedrals. Take a look at the figures of labourers carved over the front doors and the masks on the façade near the second floor that represent the world's civilizations: Asia, Africa, Europe and America. Normally tourists are not allowed inside the building but you may get a chance to see the entryway. • **233 Broadway opposite City Hall Park** Ⓢ 4, 5, 6: Brooklyn Bridge/City Hall; R, W: City Hall; 2, 3: Park Place

Wall Street (B7–8) In the middle of the 17th century, a wooden wall was erected in hopes of protecting New Amsterdam's settlers from attacks. That wall gave its name to Wall Street, one of the busiest financial centres in the world.

The area around the New York Stock Exchange is not a conventional neighbourhood; dominated by skyscrapers and office buildings it is quiet at night. But in the daytime, every nook and cranny in Wall Street is buzzing as money changes hands. • **Between Broadway and Franklin D. Roosevelt Drive** Ⓢ **2, 3, 4, 5: Wall St**

World Trade Center Site (A7–B7) The World Trade Center was a complex of seven office buildings located in Manhattan's Financial District, housing over 1,200 businesses, banks, shops, restaurants and government offices. The most famous structures in the complex were the Twin Towers, the tallest in the city at 411 m (1,350 ft). Their imposing shape dominated the lower Manhattan skyline. On September 11, 2001, the world watched with horror and disbelief as two hijacked passenger aircraft slammed into the towers, killing approximately 3,000 people. The financial district and most of the area around the site was paralyzed for weeks; the fires burned for nearly a year. Since September 11, the site where the World Trade Center stood has been nicknamed Ground Zero. An official museum and memorial are still years from opening, but a private Tribute Center which describes the history of the World Trade Center, the events of September 11 and the victims, is located on Liberty Street, directly opposite the site. On April 27, 2006, construction began on the foundations of the Freedom Tower, the cornerstone of the plan to rebuild the site. The building, designed by David Childs and Daniel Libeskind, is planned to open in 2011 or 2012. Its height will be 1776 ft (541 m), a reference to the year of the Declaration of Independence.

• **Church St between Liberty and Vesey Sts** Ⓢ **2, 3: Park Place; A, C: Broadway-Nassau; E: World Trade Center.**

◀ *A tragedy that New Yorkers, and the world with them, will never forget.*

Trinity Church (A7) This Gothic-style Episcopal church, with flying buttresses, stained-glass windows and huge bronze doors, looks oddly out of place in the bustling financial district. Consecrated in 1846, the building became so dirty over the course of the next century and a half that it was assumed to be black. When the exterior was cleaned in 1991, everyone was stunned to see that it was a rosy pink sandstone. In the spooky graveyard on the north side, the oldest gravestone is that of Richard Churcher, who died in 1681, aged five. • Mon–Fri 7am–6pm, Sat 8am–4pm, Sun 7am–4pm ☎ 1 212 602-0800 • Broadway and Wall St 🅂 J, M, Z: Broad St; N, W: Rector St; 2, 3, 4, 5: Wall St

Federal Hall National Memorial (B7) It was on the steps of Federal Hall, in 1789, that George Washington was sworn in as the first president of the United States. The Greek Revival building that currently occupies this spot was built as a US Customs House in 1842. It is now a national memorial, museum and tourist information centre. • Mon–Fri 9am–5pm ☎ 1 212 825-6888 • 26 Wall St 🅂 2, 3, 4, 5: Wall St; J, M, Z: Broad St

New York Stock Exchange (A–B7) This surprisingly small neoclassical building plays a tremendously important role in the city, both symbolically and practically. When the stock market thrives, so too does New York's reputation as the commercial hub of the US. More than 3,000 people work on the trading floor. For reasons of security, the stock exchange and its Interactive Education Center are no longer open to the public. ☎ 1 212 656-3000 • 11 Wall Street 🅂 2, 3, 4, 5: Wall St; J, M, Z: Broad St

Sports Museum of America (SmA) (A8) Baffled by the rules of baseball? Then visit this interactive, multimedia and multi-sensory museum that showcases all the sports beloved of Americans—not only baseball but also football, hockey, tennis, athletics and much more. • Daily 9am–7pm (last tickets 5.30pm) ☎ 1 212 656-3000 • 26 Broadway, entrance on Beaver St 🅂 4, 5: Bowling Green; 1, R, W: Rector St; 2, 3: Wall St; J, M, Z: Broad Street

Fraunces Tavern Museum (A8) This 18th-century tavern has been rebuilt since it was the haunt of George Washington and the Sons of Liberty. Today, besides the restaurant, there is a small museum of American History. The period rooms include the Long Room, where Washington made his farewell address to his Revolutionary War officers. • Tues–Sat noon–5pm ☎ 1 212 425-1778 • 54 Pearl St (at Broad St) Ⓢ 4, 5: Bowling Green; R, W: Whitehall St

South Street Seaport Museum (B8) This is not so much a museum as a series of exhibitions celebrating New York's deep cultural and historical roots in maritime trading, set in the heart of New York's 19th-century port district on the shore of the East River. Some buildings contain exhibits highlighting the history of shipping in New York, with galleries featuring dramatic seascape paintings. The real attraction, however, is the fleet of historic ships lined up along the dock, the largest collection of this kind in the world. • April–Oct daily (except Mon) 10am–6pm; Nov–March Fri–Mon 10am–5pm ☎ 1 212 748-8600 • 12 Fulton St Ⓢ 2, 3, 4, 5, J, M, Z: Fulton St; A, C: Broadway/ Nassau

Brooklyn Bridge (C7–8) Considered by many to be the most beautiful bridge in the world, it connects Brooklyn to Manhattan. Though construction was beset by a number of tragedies and a large death toll, it remains one of the most beloved structures in the city. The massive anchorages supporting the bridge are hollow and, for a time, the one in Manhattan was used as a cellar for storing wine; more recently, the Brooklyn anchorage was used for art exhibitions. Walk over the bridge to take in the glorious views. Ⓢ 4, 5, 6: Brooklyn Bridge/City Hall; J, M, Z: Chambers St

Vietnam Veterans Memorial (B8) Completed in 1985, this very moving memorial includes sections from veterans' letters, diary entries and poems, excerpts from speeches and reporters' dispatches from the Vietnam War, all etched into a greenish glass-brick wall. ☎ 1 212 349-1895 • 55 Water Street, Vietnam Veterans Plaza Ⓢ 1, 2, 3, 4, 5: Wall St; N, R: Whitehall St

Battery Park (A8) If you're on your way to Ellis Island or the Statue of Liberty, you'll probably go through Battery Park, the area where the original European settlers established their colony. The present-day view from the park, however, is much different from that of the 17th century. Looking south, you can see the graceful lines of the Verrazano Bridge, the docks of New Jersey, Staten Island, the Statue of Liberty, Governor's Island and Ellis Island. Behind you loom the

Brooklyn Bridge has always been an iconic part of the New York skyline.

skyscrapers of the financial district. The park contains several sculptures, most notably Fritz Koenig's *Sphere*, which once stood at the center of the Plaza at the World Trade Center. The badly damaged bronze globe is displayed along with an eternal flame. Other artworks include the Netherlands Memorial near the park entrance, *The Immigrants* sculpture near Castle Clinton, and the East Coast Memorial on the water's edge. ☎ 1 212 267-9700 • Southern tip of Manhattan Ⓢ 1: South Ferry; 4, 5: Bowling Green; R, W: Whitehall St

National Museum of the American Indian (A8) Located in the former US Customs House, this museum, a branch of the Smithsonian Institution, displays an unsurpassed collection of Native American artefacts. Highlights are feathered headdresses, weapons and silver jewellery. The murals in the rotunda are outstanding. • Daily 10am–5pm, Thurs to 8pm ☎ 1 212 514-3700 • George Gustav Heye Center, 1 Bowling Green (between Whitehall and State Sts) Ⓢ 1: South Ferry; 4, 5: Bowling Green; R, W: Whitehall St

Castle Clinton National Monument (A8) Within the 2.5-m-thick (8-ft) stone walls of this restored 19th-century fortress you'll find the kiosk for buying tickets for the ferries to the Statue of Liberty and Ellis Island as well as (rare in this part of town) well-maintained public restrooms. The castle was built in 1807, during the period leading to the War of 1812, to protect the city from encroaching British ships. • Daily 8.30am–5pm ☎ 1 212 344-7220 • Battery Park 🇸 1: South Ferry ; 4, 5: Bowling Green; R, W: Whitehall St

Museum of Jewish Heritage (A8) An exploration of the Jewish heritage and an account of the Holocaust, told from the perspective of people who experienced it firsthand.

CITY TOURS

A wealth of companies offer tours of the city by bus, helicopter or boat. All of them afford an intimate look at New York, often with live narration. Boat and helicopter tours offer the bonus of a close-up of the Statue of Liberty and Ellis Island.
Circle Line Cruise: Pier 83, W 42nd St and 12th Ave
☎ 1 212 563-3200
Spirit Cruises: Pier 62, Chelsea Piers, W 23rd St; ☎ 866 483-3866
Liberty Helicopter Tours: Heliport at Pier 6 on the East River near South Street Seaport, ☎ 1 212 967-6464

Buses reach the most interesting parts of town and many let you hop on and off.
Gray Line Sightseeing New York: Trolley Tours and Double-decker Bus Tours, 777 8th Ave, between 47th and 48th Sts
☎ 1 800 669-0051
On Location Tours: Visit places featured in TV shows and movies. www.screentours.com ☎ 1 212 209-3370.
Harlem Spirituals/New York Visions: landmark, jazz and gospel tours. 690 8th Ave, between 43rd and 44th Sts, ☎ 1 800 660-2166

Be sure to rent the award-winning audio tour. • Sun–Tues, Thurs 10am–5.45pm, Wed 10am–8pm, Fr 10am–5pm ☎ 1 646 437-4200 • 36 Battery Place ⓢ 1: South Ferry; 4, 5: Bowling Green; R, W: Whitehall St

Ellis Island Immigration Museum (map 4, J3) On the ferry to the museum, enjoy a great view of the city skyline and the Statue of Liberty. The museum opened in 1990, after extensive renovations to the building where more than 12 million immigrants entered the United States from 1892 to 1954. It features some truly moving displays spread over three floors, and you'll need at least three hours to do it justice. Exhibits include family heirlooms and photographs carried by the immigrants on their journey to America, along with letters and news stories documenting the joys, sorrows, triumphs and challenges they faced in their new homes. One of the most spectacular sights is the circular American Immigrant Wall of Honor, just outside the museum, on which the names of more than 420,000 immigrants are inscribed. • Hours change seasonally ☎ 1 212 363-3200 • Purchase tickets at Castle Clinton, daily 9.30am–5.15pm. ⓢ 4, 5: Bowling Green; 1: South Ferry; R, W: Whitehall St/South Ferry then Statue of Liberty and Ellis Island Ferry from Battery Park. Ferry information ☎ 1 212 269-5755

Statue of Liberty (map 4 J3) A symbol of freedom and opportunity, its full name is the Statue of Liberty Enlightening the World. The massive sculpture, standing more than 92 m (300 ft) above New York Harbor on Bedloes Island, was designed and built by the French sculptor Frédéric Auguste Bartholdi. Completed in Paris in 1884, the statue was presented as a gift from the French people to the United States two years later. Liberty wrests her feet free of iron shackles; her right hand raises a torch aloft, her left holds a tablet representing the Declaration of Independence. Since September 11, visitors have not been allowed inside the statue's crown but it is possible to see the interior through the glass roof of the ten-storey pedestal. Visitors are given a Monument Access pass when they buy the ferry ticket (limited numbers). ☎ 1 212 363-3200 • Purchase tickets at Castle Clinton, daily 9.30am–5.15pm or reserve on ☎ 1 87-523-9849 ⓢ 4, 5: Bowling Green; 1: South Ferry; R, W: Whitehall St/South Ferry then Statue of Liberty and Ellis Island Ferry from Battery Park. Ferry information ☎ 1 212 269-5755

WALKING TOUR: FINANCIAL DISTRICT

From Bowling Green station walk into **Battery Park**. If you want a ferry to the Statue of Liberty or Ellis Island, you can buy tickets in the round stone structure of **Castle Clinton**. Don't miss *The Sphere*, a sculpture by German artist Fritz Koenig, which stood on the plaza at the World Trade Center. It was badly damaged in the attacks and moved here unrepaired.

Walk north to the tiny **Bowling Green**, the city's first public park and the location of the **National Museum of the American Indian**. Take a moment to peek into the former US Customs House and glimpse its magnificent two-storey entry portico. Just north of Bowling Green you'll find the **Charging Bull**, a 7,000 lb bronze statue that symbolizes Wall Street's optimism.

Head north on Broadway, make a right onto Exchange Place and a left onto Broad St, and you'll be at the **New York Stock Exchange**. Visitors aren't allowed inside this building, where billions of dollars in shares are traded every day. Walk straight ahead to **Wall Street.** The statue of George Washington signals the **Federal Hall National Memorial**, where the nation's first president was inaugurated (it now contains a tourist information centre).

Go west on Wall St to Broadway. You are facing **Trinity Church**, which was the tallest structure in the city in 1846. The burial ground contains the graves of Founding Father Alexander Hamilton (1755–1804) and engineer Robert Fulton (1765–1815), who was commissioned by Napoleon to design *Nautilus*, the first submarine. Make a right, walk north to Liberty St, turn left and proceed to Church St. Behind the tall fence is the 16-acre area once occupied by the **World Trade Center**. You can gain insight into the events that transpired here by visiting 120 Liberty St, the **Tribute Center**.

Continue up Church St and make a right on Fulton St. This is **St Paul's Chapel**, the oldest public building in continuous use in Manhattan. During the collapse of the World Trade Center, the church was buried in debris but structurally undamaged. During the 260-day recovery effort, it served as a shelter for rescue workers. Today thousands of notes, banners and other items sent from around the world are displayed where workers ate, slept and prayed.

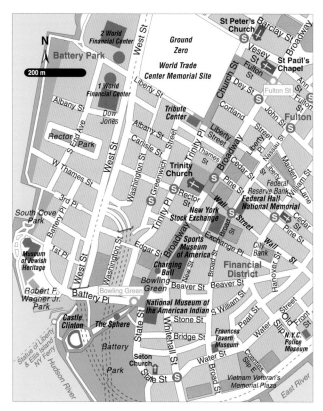

WHERE MONEY – AND HISTORY – ARE MADE

This is the oldest section of the city, once the site of the New Amsterdam settlement.

Start: Bowling Green **Finish:** St Paul's Chapel

DOWNTOWN

Each neighbourhood—SoHo, Chinatown, TriBeCa, Greenwich Village, the Lower East Side and so on—has its own special character, and often you will leave one world and enter another just by crossing the street. In terms of space, Manhattan is not a big island. In fact, you can walk from the east side of the island to the west in less than an hour, so put on your walking shoes and be on your way!

THE DISTRICT AT A GLANCE

Chinatown (C7) Until 1965, there was a strict quota on the number of Chinese allowed entry to the US, and Chinatown was a small, rather stable neighbourhood. But once the restriction was lifted, it rapidly began to expand to accommodate the most populous Chinese population in the western hemisphere, and two additional Chinatowns developed: one in Brooklyn, the other in

Queens. The oldest and most accessible is the one in Manhattan, housing 150,000–250,000 Chinese immigrants. Prepare yourself for the inescapable and seductive aromas of Asian cuisine, winding, congested streets, throngs of people, and vendors hawking everything from trinkets and toys to counterfeit videos, fresh vegetables and live fish. Steer clear of the knock-off "designer goods," which are tied to organized crime. This is an enticing neighbourhood for bargain shopping, people-watching and good, inexpensive restaurants. • Stretches north to Delancey St, south to Worth St, east to Allen St and west to Broadway **S** C, N, Q, R, M, J, W, Z, 6: Canal St; F: East Broadway

Museum of Chinese in America (B7) The leading museum dedicated to preserving and protecting the history and culture of Chinese people in the US. Opening December 2008. ☎ 1 212 619-4785 • 211–215 Centre St **S** N, R, Q, M, J, W, Z, 6: Canal St

First Shearith Israel Cemetery (C7) On the edge of Chinatown, opposite Chatham Square, this small cemetery is the oldest surviving Jewish graveyard in North America. The oldest tombstone dates from 1683. • 55–57 St James Place (between Oliver and James Sts) **S** N, R, Q, M, J, W, Z, 6: Canal St

Transfiguration Catholic Church (B7) This beautiful 200-year-old church, originally serving Irish immigrants, now has a predominantly Chinese congre-

gation. The interior is lovingly decorated. ☎ 1 212 962-5157 • 29 Mott St
Ⓢ N, R, Q, M, J, W, Z, 6: Canal St

Little Italy (B6–C7) Once a sprawling area where virtually all the residents were Italian immigrants, today Little Italy has shrunk to just a few crowded blocks. In the early and mid 20th century this area was a hotbed of mob activity and the best place in the city for genuine Italian fare, but these days the neighbourhood is primarily a place for tourists to load up on cheap trinkets and bland, greasy bowls of spaghetti. The corner of Hester and Mulberry is where infamous gangster Joey Gallo was shot down in 1972 after enjoying his last plate of scungilli at Umberto's Clam House. Martin Scorsese based much of his

STREET EATS

New York takes street food seriously. Food carts and trucks have their own web sites, newspapers review the menus, and annual "Vendy" awards go to the city's best. Keep an eye out for these favourites:
Kwik Meal (45th St and 6th Ave) for superb lamb sandwiches prepared by a white-coated chef;

Hallo Berlin (W 54th between 5th Ave and 6th Ave) with grilled sausages and German specialities;
The Famous 53rd & 6th (53rd St and 6th Ave, 7.30pm–4.00am) for halal sandwiches and platters;
NY Dosas (W 4th St and Sullivan St) with superb vegan Sri Lankan cuisine in Washington Square Park;
Super Tacos (96th St and Broadway) serves first-rate Mexican food from a shiny truck every night;

Treats Truck, which moves around the city, is a mobile bakery producing wonderful home-style cookies and brownies;
Mud Truck (7th Ave and W 4th St, 4th Ave and 8th St) serves cappuccino and latte from its bright orange fleet;
Wafels and Dinges (usually at 46th St between 5th Ave and 6th Ave) dishes up Belgian style waffles. The pastry chef who runs *Dessert Truck* (8th St and 3rd Ave) offers chocolate mousse and other restaurant-style fare.

film *Goodfellas* on his exposure to mobsters during his childhood in Little Italy. There is plenty of excellent Italian food in New York, but it is decades too late to find it here. If you feel that you must eat in Little Italy, have a snack at the cafés and pastry shops along Broome and Mulberry streets. • **Centred around Mulberry between Broome St and Canal St** Ⓢ **6: Spring St; N, R: Prince St; F, V: Broadway/Lafayette**

St Patrick's Old Cathedral (C6) Irish immigrants began construction of the cathedral in 1809. After completion in 1815 it served as the seat of the Archdiocese of New York until 1879, when the new St Patrick's on Fifth Ave replaced it. The old cathedral achieved cinematic fame as the childhood parish of Martin Scorsese and as a backdrop for several movies, including two of Francis Ford Coppola's Godfather films. ☎ **1 212 226-8075** • **263 Mulberry St on the corner of Mott and Prince** Ⓢ **6: Bleecker St; N, R: Prince St**

Children's Museum of the Arts (B6–7) A kid can arrive at the Children's Museum with no notion of art, and leave as a budding Picasso. Children aged 1 to 10 can hide in a corner with a colouring book, toss multicoloured balls into the Monet Ball Pond, or join in organized art activities. • **Wed–Sun noon–5pm, (Thurs to 6pm)** ☎ **1 212 274-0986** • **182 Lafayette St between Broome and Grand** Ⓢ **6: Spring St; R, W: Prince St**

TriBeCa (B6–7) Short for "Triangle Below Canal", TriBeCa occupies a roughly trapezoidal area. The same upper class bohemian atmosphere, elegant buildings and trendy boutiques and galleries as in SoHo, but fewer tourists and chain stores. • **Bordered by Canal St, Broadway, Barclay and the Hudson River** Ⓢ **1: Franklin St**

SoHo (B6) SoHo is short for "South of Houston". It was formerly a commercial area known as the "Cast-Iron District", with hundreds of buildings constructed in the mid-1800s to house small firms, light industries and inexpensive shops. During the 1950s many of the businesses moved out, leaving empty warehouses and factory lofts in their wake. Struggling artists moved to the neighbourhood in droves during the 1960s, converting the cheap, light-filled vacant spaces into studios and galleries. Today the rents are no longer bargains. Movie stars and models are among those who live here and frequent the salons, restaurants, cafés and boutiques. This is the place to stargaze while you eat a $5 croissant. The district has the biggest concentration of cast-iron buildings in New York. Don't miss those along Greene St, between Nos. 8 and 34, the Roosevelt Building, 478–482 Broadway and the Haughwout Building, 488–492 Broadway, location of the first Otis passenger elevator. • **Bordered by Houston St, Canal St, Crosby St, and 6th Ave** Ⓢ 6, C, E: Spring St; R, W: Prince St

New York City Fire Museum (B6) Set in a 1904 fire station, the museum displays historic firefighting equipment and traces the history of New York's bravest and best-loved heroes from the late 18th century to the present day. • Tues–Sat 10am–5pm, Sun 10am–4pm ☎ 1 212 691-1303 • **278 Spring St at Varick** Ⓢ 1: Houston St; C, E: Spring St

Greenwich Village (B–C5) The Village was once a hotbed of political activism and is the birthplace of the gay rights movement. For 150 years it was home to some of the country's most talented artists, musicians, actors and writers and has occupied an almost mythological position in American history. While most of the artists and radicals have been priced out of the area, a trendy vibe remains, due in large part to the endless stream of students at New York University, the country's largest private university. The elegant brick townhouses, the labyrinth of narrow streets, quaint and unusual stores, cafes and dimly lit bars are only a few of the reasons tourists and natives alike flock here. • **Bounded by 14th St, Houston St, the Hudson River and Broadway** Ⓢ 1: Christopher St; A, B, C, D, E, F: W 4th St/Washington Square

Church of the Ascension (C5) Completed in 1841, this Gothic Revival style brownstone structure was the first church completed on 5th Avenue, which was at the time nothing but an unpaved track. The beautiful interior is famous for its John LaFarge mural and extensive stained-glass windows. ☎ 1 212 254-8620 • **5th Ave at 10th St** Ⓢ 4, 5, 6, N, Q, R, W, L: Union Square (14th St)

Jefferson Market Library (C5) An eyeful of red stone, ornate pinnacles, towers and carvings, this landmark building is hard to miss. It houses a branch of the New

TriBeCa and SoHo are great areas for window-shopping.

York Public Library but was built in 1877 as a courthouse. ☎ 1 212 243-4334
• 425 Avenue of the Americas and 10th St Ⓢ R, W: 8th St

Washington Square Park (C5) For ad hoc performance art and a glimpse at the culture that's so much a part of Greenwich Village, you can't top Washington Square Park. In the 1600s, the Dutch used the area as a farm, and at various times it served as a cemetery and a military parade ground. Bordered by elegant homes and New York University's academic buildings, it serves as a lunch spot and social area for students and residents. Grass is sparse, but the designers included benches. If you're good at chess, stroll over to the southwest corner of the park and test your wits against a local. Washington Arch, at the northern end, was erected in 1892 in honour of the 100th anniversary of George Washington's inauguration as first president of the US. Originally built of wood, it proved so popular that it was restructured in marble (undergoing restoration).
• 5th Ave at 6th St Ⓢ A, B, C, D, E, F, V: W 4th St/Washington Square

East Village (D5–6) Peter Stuyvesant, the last Director General of the Dutch colony, had his *bouwerie* (farm) here in the 17th century. The East Village has long been a place for bold bohemian statements, and over the years radicals, students, hippies, musicians, artists and tourists have flocked here. An ever-changing mix of trash and treasure, wealth and poverty, the East Village remains full of life and flavour. • Bordered by the East River to the Bowery, from 14th St to Houston St ⑤ 6: Astor Place; L: 1st Ave; F, V: 2nd Ave

New Museum of Contemporary Art (C6) New York City's only museum devoted exclusively to contemporary art. The building is a stunning, glimmering metal mesh-clad stack of boxes designed by Tokyo-based architects Kazuyo Sejima and Ryue Nishizawa. • Sat, Sun, Wed noon–6pm, Thurs, Fri noon–10pm ☎ 1 212 219-1222 • 235 Bowery at Prince St between Stanton and Rivington Sts ⑤ 6: Spring St; N, R: Prince St. Bus M103, M6: Prince St

Tompkins Square Park (D6) Long a spot for public protests, this is also a prime place for people-watching. You'll see Eastern Europeans sharing the park with dog-walkers, young families, students, musicians, homeless people and kids from nearby public housing projects. In the centre of the park is a memorial to 1,200 women and children—mostly German immigrants from this neighbourhood—who were killed in a ferry accident on the East River in 1904. • Bordered by Ave A , Ave B, 7th and 10th Sts ⑤ 6: Astor Place; L: 1st Ave

Merchant's House Museum (C6) The city's only family home preserved intact from the 19th century, including its original furnishings and decor. Some believe the house is haunted. • Thurs–Mon noon–5pm ☎ 1 212 777-1089 • 29 E 4th St (between Lafayette and Bowery) ⑤ 6: Astor Place; N, R: 8th St; B, F: Broadway/Lafayette

St Mark's Church in the Bowery (C5) It sits on land that was once the farm of New Amsterdam's Governor Peter Stuyvesant (he and his wife are buried beneath the church). It is the city's second-oldest church, after St Paul's, being completed in 1799. The interior was turned into a versatile performance space after a fire in 1978. ☎ 1 212 674-6377 • 131 E 10th St (between 2nd and 3rd Aves) ⑤ 4, 5, 6, L, N, Q, R, S, W: 14th St/Union Square

Chelsea (B4–C4) As real estate prices skyrocketed in the West Village, young professionals began migrating north to Chelsea. These new residents mixed with the largely impoverished population, and investors soon began to see the potential. Stores were built in renovated factories, restaurants took the place of corner delis and warehouses were transformed into nightclubs. Clubs, restaurants and stores are among Chelsea's main attractions, and the area has burgeoned into a centre for the gay community. Chelsea Market at 75 Ninth Avenue between 15th and 16th Streets, is a gourmet paradise, a collection of first-rate food shops, bakeries and restaurants in a converted 1890's biscuit factory. At 222 W 23rd Street, Hotel Chelsea has long been a favourite with writers, musicians and artists. In 1978, Nancy Spungen, girlfriend of Sid Vicious of the Sex Pistols was stabbed to death in their room (later demolished) at the Chelsea. • **Bounded by the Hudson River, 5th Ave, 14th and 34th Sts** Ⓢ 1: 23rd/ 28th St; A, C, E: 23rd St

Union Square Greenmarket (C5) The city's premier greenmarket is held here year round. Chefs from the finest restaurants scour its stalls for fresh produce, cheeses, baked goods, flowers and more, from local farms. • **Mon, Wed, Fri, Sat 8am–6pm** ☎ 1 212 477-3220 • **E 17th St and Broadway** Ⓢ L, N, Q, R, W, 4, 5, 6: Union Square

Flatiron Building (C4) Completed in 1902, this triangular structure, originally the Fuller Building, was one of the city's first skyscrapers. The rounded tip at the northern end is only 2 m (6 ft) wide. • **175 5th Ave at 23rd St** Ⓢ N, R, F, V, 6: 23rd St

PARK IN THE SKY

The High Line was originally built as an elevated freight railway along the West Side of Manhattan. Although the 1.45-mile long line was intended to alleviate congestion on the streets, it was unsuccessful and abandoned after about 50 years. A few sections were demolished before plans stalled. For decades, the 22 blocks of crumbling, decaying, unused tracks were overgrown with weeds and strewn with trash. In 2001, community activists, inspired by the Promenade Plantée in Paris, convinced the authorities to have the old rail bed converted to a civic space, and the city began removing the old tracks and debris. The first section of High Line Park (open from end 2008) stretches from Gansevoort St to 20th St. The second phase, which will reach from 20th St to 30th St, is scheduled to open at the end of 2009.

WALKING TOUR: GREENWICH VILLAGE

Sheridan Square isn't a square; it is the confusing intersection of 7th Ave, W 4th, Grove and Christopher Sts. Walk east to No. 53 Christopher, the **Stonewall Inn.** On June 27, 1969, a routine police raid on this gay bar erupted into a three-day riot, sparking the gay rights movement. To commemorate the event, a sculpture entitled *Gay Liberation* stands across the street in **Christopher Park**.

Continue east on Christopher and make a right onto tiny Gay St. The basement apartment of **No. 14** was the home of writer Ruth McKenney and her beautiful sister. Ruth's stories about life here became the film *My Sister Eileen* and the musical *Wonderful Town*.

Make a right on Waverly Place, location of the triangular **Northern Dispensary**. Once a health clinic, its most famous patient was Edgar Allan Poe. Note the puzzling street sign that indicates the corner of Waverly Place and Waverly Place. Make a left onto Grove St, walk four blocks (peeking in at the lovely private garden at No. 34), turn left onto Bedford and right on Commerce St. No. 38 is the fabled **Cherry Lane Theatre**. Founded by poet Edna St Vincent Millay (she lived around the corner at 75^1/$_2$ Commerce), it has featured works by Edward Albee, Harold Pinter and Sam Shepard. Follow the curving street and turn left onto Barrow St.

You can glimpse the private courtyard garden at 72 Barrow just before you turn right on Hudson St. Opposite, at 487 Hudson, is **St Luke in the Fields**, founded in 1820. One of first wardens of this Episcopal Church was Clement Clarke Moore, author of *Twas the night before Christmas*.

Make a right onto Grove St. Halfway up the block is **Grove Court**, the most exclusive street in the Village. Only homeowners have keys that open its always-secure gate.

Make a left onto Bedford and continue until the street ends at Christopher. The sidewalk outside the **Lucille Lortel Theatre** at No. 121 indicates the playwrights whose work has been performed there, including Tennessee Williams and Athol Fugard. Walk east to No. 81, site of **St John's Evangelical Lutheran Church** and **Hartwick Seminary**. Founded in 1792, this was the first Lutheran Theological Seminary in the US. A few steps east return you to Sheridan Square.

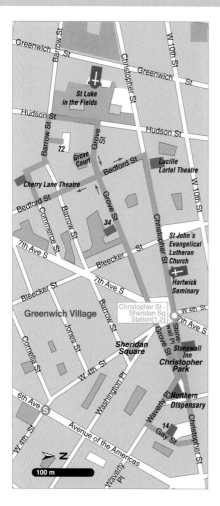

OFFBEAT AND OFF THE BEATEN PATH

Many of the legendary spots that made the fame of the Village have closed down. This walk takes you through a mostly residential area where it is still possible to experience the low-key, charming neighborhood that once served as a magnet for artists and radicals.

Start and Finish: Sheridan Square

READ ALL ABOUT IT

Whether they are riding on the subway, sunbathing on a rooftop or sitting on a park bench, New Yorkers are nearly always reading. It's no wonder the city has so many unique, quirky bookstores. Here are some of the best.

Stores that specialize in books on a single topic include the **Drama Book Shop**, a bookstore for theatre lovers that even has a resident theatre company (250 W 40th St between 7th and 8th Aves ☎ 1 212 944-0595); and the **Mysterious Bookshop**, selling only mystery, crime, espionage and detective fiction (58 Warren St between W Broadway and Church St ☎ 1 212 587-1011).

Open-minded readers flock to **Bluestockings Books**, a radical feminist bookstore and fair-trade vegan café on the Lower East Side (172 Allen St between Stanton and Rivington ☎ 1 212 777-6028); and the **Oscar Wilde Bookshop**, the world's oldest gay and lesbian bookstore (15 Christopher St at 6th Ave ☎ 1 212 255-8097).

Books meant to enlighten are offered at **Quest Bookshop** which specializes in volumes on ancient and new spiritual beliefs including Wicca, astrology and tarot (240 E 53rd St at 2nd Ave, ☎ 1 212 758-5521); and **East-West Books**, a shop that combines spiritual, holistic health and metaphysical books with a vegetarian café and yoga lessons (78 Fifth Ave at 14th St ☎ 1 212 243-5994).

You can't find a better second-hand-book seller than **Housing Works Used Book Café**, which offers books, CDs and fresh baked goods on a back street in SoHo. All profits from this charity-fun shop are used to help homeless people with AIDS and HIV. (126 Crosby St ☎ 1 212 334-3324).

When you want to read fantasy, try **Books of Wonder**, specializing in children's literature both classic and new, including old, rare, and out-of-print editions (18 W 18th St at 6th Ave ☎ 1 212 989-3270). **Forbidden Planet** is known for its huge collection of science fiction, fantasy, comic books and graphic novels (840 Broadway at 13th St ☎ 1 212 473-1576).

You can begin to plan your next trip at the **Complete Traveller Bookstore**, an antiquarian bookseller specializing in travel books with an extensive collection of Baedeker's guides (199 Madison Ave at 35th St ☎ 1 212 685-9007).

BookCourt is Brooklyn's most beloved bookstore, offering a friendly, personal service with an exceptional selection of works by local authors, many of whom are also customers (163 Court St near Pacific St ☎ 1 718 875-3677)

Finally, no reader should visit New York without seeing the **Strand Bookstore**. Famed as the world's biggest bookstore, its shelves hold more than 18 miles of used and new books (828 Broadway at 12th St ☎ 1 212 473-1452).

New York in Books

Some titles you might enjoy:
Wonderful Town: New York Stories from The New Yorker, David Remnick;
The Hidden Chorus: Poetry and Fiction, NY Writers Coalition;
Writing New York: A Literary Anthology, Phillip Lopate;
New York Stories: The Best of the City Section of the New York Times, Connie Rosenblum;
The Great Bridge, David McCullough;
Here is New York, E.B. White;
The Island at the Center of the World, Russell Shorto;
The City Beneath Us: Building the New York Subway, New York Transit Museum;
Along the Way: MTA Arts for Transit, Sandra Bloodworth and William Ayres.

And for children:
You Can't Take a Balloon into the Metropolitan Museum, Jacqueline Preiss Weitzman;
This is New York, Miroslav Saske;
Tar Beach, Faith Ringgold;
A Tree Grows in Brooklyn, Betty Smith.

MIDTOWN

Spanning the area from the Hudson River to the East River, Midtown is the shopping, dining, theatre-going, people-watching heart of New York. You can find almost anything in Midtown if you don't mind the hustle and bustle of the city's busiest intersections.

THE DISTRICT AT A GLANCE

Madison Square Garden (C4) The premier sports arena in the city, whether you are a Knicks or Rangers fan. Also a favourite concert venue and site of the Westminster Kennel Club Dog Show. ☎ 1 212 465-6741 • 2 Penn Plaza (at 33rd St and 7th Ave) Ⓢ A, C, E, 1, 2, 3: 34th St

Empire State Building (D4) Built in 1931, the 381-m (1,250-ft) structure (not counting the TV tower) reigned as the world's tallest skyscraper until the 1970s. One of the city's most beloved landmarks, it is the stuff of legends and

How many skyscrapers in Manhattan? Go to the top of the Empire State Building and start counting!

drama. In 1933, King Kong made his way to the top on film screens; on a foggy day in July 1945, an Army B-25 crashed into the 79th floor, killing 14 people; in 1986 a couple of British tourists parachuted from the 86th floor. Today, some 3.5 million visitors make their way to the observation decks on the 86th and 102nd floors, from where you can see all Manhattan and the four outer boroughs. To beat the crowds, get there early. The New York Skyride, on the second floor, is a flight-simulator that takes you on an airborne tour of the city. The floodlights atop the building change color to match holidays and special events; they are green on St Patrick's Day, red and green at Christmas, lavender for the Gay Pride parade. • Daily 8am–2am; last elevators go up at 1.15am ☎ 1 212 736-3100; New York Sykride ☎ 1 212 279-9777 • 350 5th Ave at 34th St **S** N, R, B, D, F, Q: Herald Square/34th St

Morgan Library and Museum (D3) The collection includes illuminated and historical manuscripts, early printed books, and old master drawings and prints.

Exhibits have focused on everything from Gutenberg Bibles to Bob Dylan's handwritten notes. • Tues–Thurs 10.30am–5pm, Fri 10.30am–9pm, Sat 10am–6pm, Sun 11am–6pm ☎ 1 212 685-0008 • 225 Madison Ave at 36th St ⑤ 6: 33rd St; 4, 5, 6, 7: Grand Central; B, D, F, Q: 42nd St

United Nations (E4) Once you set foot in the United Nations, you are technically no longer in New York, or even in the US. The entire area between 42nd and 48th Sts on 1st Ave is international territory. There's much to see here: flags representing each member nation, the Secretariat and General Assembly buildings, the Dag Hammarskjöld Library (named after the UN Secretary-General killed when his plane exploded in 1961 during a peace mission to Congo) and the Conference Building. If you want to join a tour (leaving every 30 min from the General Assembly lobby, call ahead and arrive early, as they often sell out. You can enjoy the wonderful landscaped garden without a guide. • Mon–Fri 9.30am–4.45pm ☎ 1 212 963-8687 • 1st Ave at 46th St ⑤ 4, 5, 6, 7, S: Grand Central Terminal/42nd St. Bus M15, M27

Chrysler Building (D4) During the first half of the 20th century, architects feverishly competed to build the city's tallest structure; the press called it the Race into the Sky. In 1929, H. Craig Severance unveiled the 283-m (927-ft) Bank of Manhattan and thought he'd won. But a few days later a large steel spire was hoisted on top of the building William Van Alen built as headquarters for the Chrysler Automobile Corporation, giving it a total height of 319 m (1,048 ft), that eclipsed Severance's structure. You can't go past the beautifully appointed Art Deco lobby, but be sure to see the wood-covered elevator doors. And you can't help but admire the steel exterior, eagle gargoyles and gleaming spire, modelled on a radiator grille. ☎ 1 212 682-3070 • 405 Lexington Ave between 42nd and 43rd Sts ⑤ 4, 5, 6, 7, S: 42nd St

Grand Central Terminal (D3) Not everyone who works in Manhattan lives there, and those who commute from the Northern suburbs go through Grand Central Terminal. What has so intrigued visitors and natives alike is that engineers managed to bring a bustling railway system into the heart of one of the busiest cities in the world—and do it silently and invisibly through tunnels. It is crowned by a beautiful Beaux Arts structure. The better part of the station is taken up by the main concourse, through which 500,000 commuters pass daily. The ceiling depicts the constellations, backwards. The artist, Frenchman Paul Helleu, was inspired by a medieval manuscript. In 1997 it was fully cleaned and restored to its original blue colour. Three intricate sculptures, a massive clock and a row of arched windows grace the terminal's southern facade. Don't miss the tourist information window in the Main Concourse and dining concourse on the lower level. • **Free tours every Wed at 12.30pm; meet at the center information booth on the Main Concourse. Private guided tours can be booked 2–3 weeks in advance on** ☎ 1 212 340-2347 • E 42nd St at Park Ave 🚇 4, 5, 6, 7, S: Grand Central Terminal/42nd St

New York Public Library (D3) One of the best places to observe this city in perpetual motion is on the steps of the main branch of the New York Public Library. Take a seat between the two marble lions dubbed "Patience" and "Fortitude" and watch Manhattan's theatre unfold. With its 15 million items, including the original Winnie the Pooh, a Gutenberg bible and ancient Japanese scrolls, the library is widely renowned as one of the pre-eminent research facilities in the world. Free

Internet access is provided in the cavernous Rose Reading Room. To see the main attractions, join a free guided tour. • **Library open Mon, Thurs, Fri, Sat 11am–6pm; Tues, Wed, 11am–7.30pm; Sun 1pm–5pm. Guided tours Mon–Sat 11am and 2pm, Sun 2pm** ☎ 1 212 340-0833 • 455 5th Ave between 40th and 42nd Sts 🚇 4, 5, 6, 7, B, D, F, Q, S, V: 42nd St

Bryant Park (D3) Adjacent to the New York Public Library, this midtown park is named after poet and editor William Cullen Bryant. A green oasis surrounded by skyscrapers, it is a perfect place to enjoy an outdoor meal with the business people who use the park as a lunch spot. There's a restaurant and café, as well as free Internet access. In summer the lawn is popular with sunbathers and the carousel with children. There are areas for chess and pétanque players, and readers are provided with free books and periodicals. In winter the lawn is converted to a free ice skating rink, and a holiday gift market is erected around the fountain. The park sits over a vast underground facility housing part of library's extensive collections. • **Bordered by 42nd and 40th Sts, between 5th and 6th Aves 🚇** 7, B, D, F, V: 42nd St

Intrepid Sea-Air-Space Museum (B2) This massive aircraft carrier, with a crew of 3,000, was commissioned in 1942 for service in World War II. The NASA used it to recover space capsules. After serving in the Vietnam War, the Intrepid was transformed into a museum. • **Scheduled to re-open November 2008 after renovation** ☎ 1 212 245-0072 www.intrepidmuseum.org • **Pier 86 on the Hudson River, W 46th St and 12th Ave 🚇** A, C, E, 1, 2, 3, 7, 9, N, R, Q, S, W: Times Square, then transfer to M42 West bus

International Center of Photography (D3) Founded in 1974 by Cornell Capa to safeguard the work of his brother Robert, a well-known photojournalist killed by a landmine in Vietnam in 1954, the Center also houses a school. The exhibitions generally carry a humanitarian and/or political message. Also retrospectives on master photographers. The gift shop contains a wide selection of books, posters and postcards. • **Tues–Thurs 10am–6pm; Fri 10am–8pm; Sat, Sun 10am–6pm** ☎ 1 212 857 0000 • **1133 Avenue of the Americas at 43rd St 🚇** B, D, F, V: 42nd St/Bryant Park; 1, 2, 3, 7, N, Q, R, S, W: Times Square/42nd St. Bus M5, M6, M7: 42nd St

Times Square (D3) No, it isn't square, nor is it still the home of the *New York Times* (based for many years in the tower at No. 1), the newspaper after which it was named. Once known as a gritty, slightly dangerous destination, today's Times Square is a bright, shiny, family-friendly shopping and entertainment district. Few places are quite as exciting or overwhelming. The glittering,

Giant baubles brighten up Rockefeller Plaza for the Christmas season.

animated signs rival those of Las Vegas and, if you're looking for tickets to Broadway shows, cheap souvenirs, pricey fast food and aggressive hucksters, this is the place to go. Many well-known brands operate massive, multi-storey shops here, including Virgin, MTV, Swatch, Sephora, McDonald's and Disney.
⑤ N, Q, R, S, W, 1, 2, 3, 7: Times Square/42nd St

Rockefeller Center (D3) An Art-Deco masterpiece in the heart of midtown, this is a giant complex of office buildings, theatres, underground pedestrian passageways and shops, created by John D. Rockefeller in 1929. Almost 300,000 people work in or visit the Center every day. The main attractions are the Channel Gardens (just off 5th Ave between 49th and 50th Sts), so-called because they separate the British Empire Building from the Maison Française, the huge gilded bronze statue of *Prometheus* in the sunken Lower Plaza that serves as an outdoor café during the summer and an ice-skating rink throughout the winter, the furniture and frescoes of Radio City Music Hall

(America's largest indoor theatre), the General Electric Building (home to the NBC television network) and, for game-players, the well-stocked Nintendo store. NBC-TV's popular *Today* program is broadcast live from the Plaza every morning. Check out the Center's huge Christmas tree if you are in New York in December. ☎ 1 212 632-3975 • 5th to 7th Aves and 47th to 50th Sts ⑤ B, D, F, V: 47th–50th Sts/Rockefeller Center

Top of the Rock (D3) The observation deck on the 70th floor of the Rockefeller Center offers a great view of the city. • Daily 8am–midnight; last elevator 11pm ☎ 1 212 698-2000 • 30 Rockefeller Plaza ⑤ B, D, F, V: 47th–50th Sts/Rockefeller Center

Christie's New York (D3) A fascinating view of the world of high-stakes, international auctioning. In May 2008, Monet's *Railroad Bridge at Argenteuil* sold here for $41.4 million. • Mon–Fri 9.30am–5.30pm ☎ 1 212 636-2000 • 20 Rockefeller Plaza at 49th St ⑤ B, D, F, V: Rockefeller Center

Radio City Music Hall (D3) This has been the city's largest and most noteworthy theatre ever since it was completed in 1932. The vast auditorium and stage are home to the beloved Rockettes, a troupe of glamorous precision dancers with their signature eye-high kicks, presenting fabulous holiday and seasonal theatrical dance entertainments. • Tours of the building daily 11am–3pm ☎ 1 212 307-7171 • 1260 Avenue of the Americas (at 50th St) ⑤ B, D, F, V: Rockefeller Center

◀ *No visitor could complain that there's a lack of entertainment!*

St Patrick's Cathedral (D3) Home to the Roman Catholic Archdiocese of New York and a symbol of the influence and success of Irish immigrants in the US, St Patrick's Cathedral sits elegantly amid the skyscrapers of midtown. The land on which the cathedral is built was originally destined to be a cemetery, but the ground proved far too rocky for burials, so in 1850 Archbishop John Hughes announced his plans to build a cathedral "worthy of God, worthy of the Catholic religion, and an honor to this great city". Because of the Civil War, construction was not completed until 1879. • Daily 6.30am–8.45pm. Tours available, phone in advance for the schedules ☎ 1 212 753-2261• 5th Ave at 51st St ⑤ B, D, F, Q, V: 47th–50th Sts/Rockefeller Center; E: 53rd St; 6: 51st St

Paley Center for Media (D3) There's a growing school of thought that contemporary American culture owes more to television than literature, theatre and music combined. This museum, formerly known as the Museum of Television and Radio, will convince you it's true. There's a collection of more than 140,000 programs covering almost 100 years of television and radio history and an array of consoles where you can watch and listen. • Tues, Wed, Fri–Sun noon–6pm, Thurs noon–8pm ☎ 1 212 621-6800 • 25 W 52nd St ⑤ E, V: 5th Ave; N, R, W; 49th St; B, D, F, V: 47th–50th Sts

Museum of Modern Art (D3) MoMA is light, airy and dynamic, filled with countless paintings, sculptures, drawings, prints and photographs as well as masterpieces of modern film and design. Every period of modern art, from Expressionism to Op Art, Dadaism to Surrealism, is represented. Dali's *Persistence of Memory*, Chagall's *Birthday*, Picasso's *Les Demoiselles d'Avignon*, Van Gogh's *Starry Night*, Warhol's *Campbell's Soup Cans* are among the famous paintings on display. Together with the rest of the 150,000 piece collection, they tell the story of modern art and make MoMA a must-see. There are also sections of prints and illustrated books. Two theatres accommodate the Film and Media programmes. The 6-storey building includes two casual cafes and a formal restaurant next to the Sculpture Garden. • Wed, Thurs, Sat–Mon 10.30am–5.30pm, Fri 10.30am–8pm ☎ 1 212 708-9400 • 11 W 53rd St, between 5th and 6th Aves ⑤ E, V: 5th Ave; B, D, F, V: 47th–50th Sts/Rockefeller Center. Bus M1, 2, 3, 4, 5: 53rd St

Figuring out Ellsworth Kelly's Colors for a Large Wall *(1951) in the MoMA.*

Trump Tower (D3) Even if you're not going to buy anything in its pricey shops, it is worth stepping inside to see the 5-level atrium (complete with waterfall) of the Trump Tower, the flashy, gilded flagship of controversial real-estate developer Donald Trump. The tower's 58 storeys house shops, cafés, offices and apartments; the public spaces are clad in a white-veined pink marble with brass and mirrors throughout. ☎ 1 212 832-2000 • 725 5th Ave at 56th St Ⓢ E, V: 53rd St; N, R, W: 5th Ave/59th St

PaceWildenstein (E3) PaceWildenstein handles the works of many of the world's best-known contemporary artists: paintings, photographs, drawings and sculptures by Alexander Calder, Jean Dubuffet, Henry Moore, Claes Oldenburg, Pablo Picasso, Mark Rothko, Kiki Smith, Isamu Noguchi and more. • Tues–Fri 9.30am–6pm; Sat 10am–6pm ☎ 1 212 421-3292 • 32 E 57th St, 2nd Floor. Other galleries downtown at 534 W 25th St and 545 W 22nd St Ⓢ N, R, W: 5th Ave

WALKING TOUR: TIMES SQUARE FOR CHILDREN

Begin on the northeast corner of 8th Ave and 42nd St, and look up to see the colourful, curved walls of the **Westin Hotel**. Critics have called it the ugliest building in New York, but kids love its brightly colour and geometric shapes.

Walk east along 42nd St to No. 234, where two big, glitzy entertainment centres stand side by side: a branch of **Madame Tussaud's**, with painstakingly created wax figures including Superman, Oprah Winfrey, David Beckham and Paris Hilton, and **Ripley's Believe it or Not Odditorium**. Most of the items displayed come from the collection of Robert Ripley, a real-life Indiana Jones who travelled the world collecting the bizarre and unusual including shrunken heads, mummies and an albino giraffe.

Across the street, at No. 233, is the **Sanrio** store, bursting with products from this Japanese purveyor of cuteness, best known for its Hello Kitty character. A few steps east, at No. 209, you'll find the **New Victory Theater**. This, New York's oldest active theatre, has been refitted for young audiences. Its first-rate international productions, ranging from puppetry to circus acts, are carefully selected to appeal to even first-time theater-goers.

Proceed to the corner and turn left onto 7th Avenue. At 43rd St, the **Hard Rock Café** is housed in the former Paramount Theatre, where the Beatles and Elvis Presley once performed and their memorabilia is now exhibited.

Continue north and cross to Broadway and 44th for **Toys R Us**, a massive toy shop that contains a full-sized Ferris wheel that you can ride, a two-storey Barbie dollhouse, the New York skyline in Legos and a 34-ft Jurassic Park T-Rex dinosaur that roars.

A block north, on the corner of Broadway and 45th, is the neon-fronted **Virgin Megastore**, with three levels of CDs, DVDs, listening posts and T-shirts. Go straight up Broadway to 48th St, where two rival candy companies, **Hershey's** and **M&M's**, have seet up their shops across the street from each other. Either will provide a sweet ending to your tour around Times Square.

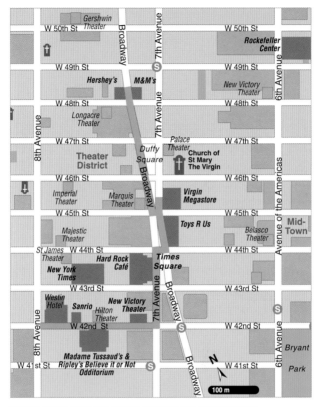

FAMILY ENTERTAINMENT AT THE CROSSROADS OF THE WORLD

Times Square, once the city's seedy side, is now the cleaned, renovated and child-friendly heart of New York.

Start: 8th Ave and 42nd St **Finish:** Broadway and 48th St

SHOPPER'S PARADISE

Whatever you want, you can find it in New York. As befits a shopping mecca, all the big shops (and many of the smaller places) are open seven days a week and well into the evening.

Department Stores

The big, full-service stores in Midtown carry a wide variety of goods—everything from cosmetics to towels—and most include in-store restaurants, salons and cafés. The big four are **Macy's** (151 W 34th St at Herald Square), **Lord & Taylor** (424 5th Ave at 39th St), **Bloomingdales** (1000 3rd Ave at 59th St) and **Saks Fifth Ave** (611 5th Ave at 49th St).

Designer Shops

Premier luxury stores are clustered in three locations, all ready to tempt your taste and your credit card. In Lenox Hill (Madison Ave from 60th to 77th Streets), you'll find Barney's, Hermès, Calvin Klein, Dolce & Gabbana, Giorgio Armani, Chloe, Fendi and many others.

Just south of Central Park, near the intersection 57th St and 5th Ave, this area near Trump Tower contains Henri Bendel, Takashimaya, Christian Dior, Burberry, Prada, Louis Vuitton, Bergdorf Goodman, YSL, Gucci, Armani, Escada and much, much more.

Head downtown to SoHo for Chanel, Betsey Johnson, Charles Jourdan, DKNY, Marc Jacobs, Helmut Lang, Anna Sui and many emerging designers.

Jewellery

Midtown Manhattan is home of the world's largest shopping district for diamonds and fine jewellery. The block of W 47th St between Fifth Avenue and Avenue of the Americas is known as the **Diamond District**. Close

to 3,000 jewellers are here, most working in booths within the marketplaces known as exchanges. Haggling is welcome and expected here.

Many fine jewellers are located around 5th Avenue and 57th Street. Within a few blocks are elegant shops for Tiffany, Cartier, Van Cleef & Arpel, Harry Winston, DeBeers, H. Stern, Bulgari, Mikimoto, Dunhill and Piaget.

Antiques

If you're looking for high-quality antiques, try **Dalva Brothers** (53 E 77th St) who sell 18th-century decorative arts to museums, **James Robinson, Inc.**, (480 Park Ave at 58th St) with its outstanding collection of antique jewellery, silver flatware, glass and porcelain or the **Manhattan Art and Antiques Center** (1050 2nd Ave at 56th St) which has over 100 dealers representing every category of arts and antiquities.

Flea Markets

Open on weekends only, open-air Flea markets offer antiques, vintage items and interesting junk. You can browse, haggle and have fun at the **Annex/ Hell's Kitchen Flea Market** (39th St between 9th and 10th Ave), **Green Flea Market No.1** (Columbus Ave between 76th and 77th Sts) or **Green Flea Market No. 2** (PS 41, 34 Greenwich Ave at Charles St).

UPTOWN

The stretch of Manhattan from 59th all the way to the northern tip of the island. The sections to the left and right of Central Park are called the Upper West Side and the Upper East Side and have different flavours; see them both and decide if you have a preference.

THE DISTRICT AT A GLANCE

Central Park (D2–E1 and map 3) This 340-ha (843-acre) stretch of paths, ponds, trees and grass is as elemental to New Yorkers as water and air. Transformed from swampy wastelands, it is the fruit of a massive project that began in 1857 and took 20 years to complete. There is no end to the list of things you can do here. Hop on a horse-drawn carriage (known as a Hansom Cab) at Central Park South for a cosy tour. In summer, you can copy the New Yorkers

Frederick Law Olmsted and Calvert Vaux designed Central Park as a place where people from all walks of life could relax and meditate.

who flock to the vast Sheep Meadow to throw frisbees and sunbathe, play tennis on one of the park's 26 clay courts, rollerblade along the 72nd St transverse, visit the zoo, or take in a free performance. During the winter, you can slip on a pair of ice skates at Wollman Rink and perfect your pirouette. Don't miss the lake and Loeb Boathouse, where you can rent rowboats and bicycles or have a snack at the Boathouse Café. Another highlight is Strawberry Fields, Yoko Ono's tribute to her husband John Lennon, featuring an English-style garden and the iconic "Imagine" mosaic. The Conservatory Garden, about a mile north of the Reservoir, is one of the most beautiful, tranquil niches in the park. **S** A, B, C, D, 1: 59th St; F, Q: 57th St; N, R, W: 5th Av/59th St

Upper East Side (E1–F2, map 3 D–E1–5) Many of the American industrialists who made their fortunes in the 19th century built mansions in this clean, safe and tidy rectangle of streets: Andrew Carnegie, Henry Frick, and Cornelius Vanderbilt once called the Upper East Side home. Most of the New Yorkers living here today share a reputation for being cultured, sophisticated and a bit snobbish. Don't miss the Gracie Mansion at East End Ave and 88th St, the Carlyle Hotel at 76th St and Madison Ave, and the luxury boutiques along Lexington and Madison Aves. • Bordered by 59th St, 5th Ave, the East River and 96th St ⊖ 4, 5, 6: 59th/ 86th Sts; F: Lexington Ave/63rd St

Queensboro Bridge (F3) If you're a fan of the intricacies of bridge construction, make a detour to 59th St and 1st Ave, preferably at sunset, for a close-up of the Queensboro Bridge, a painting come to life. The 360-m (1,182-ft) steel span links Queens and Manhattan and is used by cars, cyclists and pedestrians. The Bridge, which was completed in 1909, was immortalized in a popular song by Simon & Garfunkel and is the setting for a dramatic scene in the 2002 film, *Spider-Man.* ⊖ 4, 5, 6, B, R, W: 59th St

Frick Collection (E2, map 3 D4) The Frick Collection is housed in one of the most elegant mansions on Fifth Ave. The collection of European paintings (most of them dating from the Renaissance to the late 19th century) rivals that of any major art museum. Titian's *Man in a Red Cap*, Gainsborough's *Sarah, Lady Innes*, Rembrandt's *Portrait of a Young Artist* and Vermeer's *Mistress and Maid* are only a few of the dozens of masterpieces that Henry Clay Frick, who made his fortune in the steel industry, hung on the walls of his home. There's also a fascinating collection of antique furniture, drawings, porcelains and a delightful indoor courtyard with a fountain. • Tues–Sat 10am–6pm, Sun 11am–5pm ☎ 1 212 288-0700 • 1 E 70th St ⊖ 6: 68th St. Bus: uptown via Madison Ave, downtown via 5th Ave

Knoedler & Co. (E2, map 3 D 4) Knoedler is America's establishment gallery, one of the oldest in the United States, having celebrated its 160th anniversary. It currently specializes in post-war and contemporary art with a focus on the New York School, and represents Milton Avery, Herbert Ferber and Frank Stella, among others. • Tues–Fri 9.30am–5.30pm; Sat 10am–5.30pm ☎ 1 212 794-0550 • 19 E 70th St ⊖ 6: 68th St

Whitney Museum of American Art (E2, map 3 D 4) The eccentric socialite Gertrude Vanderbilt Whitney offered her collection to the Metropolitan Museum of Art in 1929, but they turned her down. Two years later, with a vast inheritance in hand, she opened her own museum. Today it houses the most important assemblage of 20th-century American art in the country. Every notable American artist working during this period is represented in the 12,000-piece permanent collection, including Edward Hopper, Jackson Pollock, Jasper Johns, Georgia O'Keeffe, Roy Lichtenstein and Frank Stella. Restaurant and gift shop. • Wed–Thurs, Sat –Sun 11am–6pm, Fri 1–9pm ☎ 1 212 570-3600 or 1 800 944-8639 • 945 Madison Ave at 75th St Ⓢ 6: 77th St. Bus: uptown via Madison Ave, downtown via 5th Ave

Carl Schurz Park (off map by F1) Stretching along the East River, this park is one of the quietest in the city and offers lovely views of the river and its traffic. It is also the site of Gracie Mansion, the mayor's official residence and one of the oldest surviving wooden structures in Manhattan. • East End Ave at E 86th St Ⓢ 4, 5, 6: 86th St

Metropolitan Museum of Art (E1, map 3 D3) "The Met" is the gem of all American museums, its works a showcase of artistic excellence throughout the history of mankind. Exhibits of European master painters, Roman and Greek sculptors, Chinese calligraphers, African instrument-makers and Egyptian jewellers make up only a small part of the museum's vast collection. Where do you start? Go to the Information Desk for maps, brochures and tour schedules. Some of the exhibits that have been enthralling visitors since the museum opened here in 1880 include a 14,000-piece collection of arms and armour, featuring swords, helmets and arrowheads. The American Wing traces the development of American interior design and decorative arts over the last four centuries. The medieval art collection includes a stunning display of rare 15th-century tapestries. The galleries in the 19th-century European Paintings and Sculpture section house works by Goya, Rousseau, Rodin, Manet, Cezanne and Degas. Among the musical instruments are rare violins, the oldest existing piano, a jade flute, sitars and gongs. The Met's gift shop is second to none, with an endless selection of posters, games, jewellery and art books. In summer and fall the roof garden at sunset is a must. • Tues–Thurs, Sun 9.30am–5.30pm, Fri–Sat to 9pm ☎ 1 212 535-7710 • 1000 Fifth Ave at 82nd St Ⓢ 4, 5, 6: 86th St. Bus: uptown via Madison Ave, downtown via 5th Ave

Guggenheim Museum (E1, map 3 D2) The building itself—designed by Frank Lloyd Wright—has attracted almost as much commentary as the works of art inside. Some critics say the museum looks like a giant toilet, others insist it was Wright's most ingenious design. The exhibition space is shaped liked a spiral, with a curved ramp leading from the ground floor to the top of the building. The idea is to view the works in one continuous line. The permanent collection includes significant works by Brancusi, Cézanne, Chagall, Kandinsky, Klee, Léger, Picasso, Rauschenberg, and more. You can find some great bargains in posters in the museum gift shop. • Sat–Wed 10am–5.45pm, Fri to 7.45pm ☎ 1 212 423-3500 • 1071 5th Ave at 89th St ⑤ 4, 5, 6: 86th St. Bus: uptown via Madison Ave, downtown via 5th Ave

Cooper-Hewitt Museum (map 3 D2) The landmark 64-room house of industrialist Andrew Carnegie, built in 1902, is now the National Museum of Design, housing a collection of product designs and decorative arts, drawings, engravings, wallcoverings and a remarkable assortment of Egyptian, Near Eastern and Mediterranean fabrics dating back to the 3rd century.

◀ *A matter of taste: the design of the Guggenheim draws mixed reactions.*

Watch your head as you go through the doors: Carnegie was only 5 ft 2 in tall and built the mansion to his own requirements. • Mon–Thurs 10am–5pm, Fri to 9pm, Sun noon–6pm ☎ 1 212 849-8400 • 2 E 91st St Ⓢ 4, 5, 6: 86th/96th Sts. Bus: Uptown via Madison Ave, downtown via 5th Ave

Jewish Museum (map 3 D2) Memorable, moving and educational, the museum demonstrates how Jewish culture is reflected in art. The collection includes archaeological objects, ingenious multi-media installations and an enormous collection of broadcast media, drawings, prints and sculptures. • Sat–Wed 11am–5.45pm; Thurs to 8pm; closed on Fri, free admission Sat ☎ 1 212 423-3200 • 1109 5th Ave at 92nd St Ⓢ 4, 5, 6: 86th St. Bus: uptown via Madison Ave, downtown via 5th Ave

Museum of the City of New York (map 3 D1) The place to explore the history of New York City from the earliest days to the present. Among the highlights are the theatre, toy, costume and photography collections and the exhibition detailing 17th-century Dutch life in New York. The museum also sponsors a limited number of excellent walking tours around the city; call for information and reservations. • Tues–Sun 10am–5pm ☎ 1 212 534-1672 • 1220 5th Ave between 103rd and 104th Sts Ⓢ 6: 103rd St; 2, 3: 110th St. Bus: uptown via Madison Ave, downtown via 5th Ave

El Museo del Barrio (map 3 D1) One of the most underrated museums in New York, it began as a simple display in a school classroom in East Harlem but now counts some 8,000 paintings, photographs, sculptures and artefacts, including the magnificent *santos de palo* carvings. This is the only museum in the nation devoted entirely to the culture of Puerto Rico and Latin America. It radiates an unmistakable feeling of fellowship and warmth. • Galleries scheduled to re-open in autumn 2009 after renovation ☎ 1 212 831-7272 www.elmuseo.org • 1230 5th Ave at 104th St Ⓢ 6: 103rd St; 2, 3: 110th St. Bus: uptown via Madison Ave, downtown via 5th Ave

Upper West Side (C1–D2, map 3 A–B1–5) Once East Siders were likely to tell you that West Siders are liberal and unreasonable, and West Siders would retort that East Siders are conservative and greedy. But these days, the areas are very much alike: wealthy, sophisticated and exclusive. Elegant apartment buildings and townhouses and up-market boutiques line the avenues and cross streets. The Beatle John Lennon lived in the Dakota Building on Central Park West and 72nd St; he was murdered on the sidewalk in front of his home in December 1980. • Bounded by the Hudson River, Central Park, 59th and 125th Sts ❺ 1, 2, 3: 79th St

Lincoln Center (D2, map 3 D2) The Lincoln Center for the Performing Arts is awe-inspiring in its comprehensive cultural offerings. Encompassing opera, ballet, theatre, symphony and film in its many and various theatres, it should figure on any visitor's itinerary. The fountain in the centre of the plaza is a great spot for people-watching and taking in the grandeur of the setting. The Center contains a total of 12 arts organizations including schools, theatres, concert halls and libraries. If you are standing at the fountain, the grand building directly ahead is the Metropolitan Opera. To your right is the Avery Fisher Hall, home of the New York Philharmonic and the city's premier concert location; to your left is the New York State Theater, home of the City Ballet and the City Opera. One block further uptown, not directly on the plaza, is the Alice Tully Hall, a concert hall for recitals, chamber music and small-scale opera (scheduled to re-open February 2009). ☎ 1 212 875-5456 • 62nd St and Columbus Ave ❺ 1: 66th St Lincoln Center

American Museum of Natural History (E1, map 3 B3) The beauties and intricacies of the world's inhabitants—from the first invertebrates to modern man—are underlined in this fascinating museum, which children will love, too. Have a good look at the most minute details of a jellyfish, the hair on the back of a hyena, the teeth of a prehistoric shark and the face paint on an Indian warrior. The museum is best known for its Dinosaur Halls filled with massive fossils, the dioramas that show wild animals in their natural habitats, and the Rose Center, a monumental, high-tech planetarium. You can also admire the Star of India—a 563-carat sapphire found 300 years ago in Sri Lanka and the largest known to man. • Daily 10am–5.45pm (the Rose Center stays open until 8.45pm on the first Friday of the month) ☎ 1 212 769-5100 • 79th St and Central Park West ❺ 1: W 79th; B, C: 81st St. Bus: Uptown via Amsterdam Ave, downtown via Columbus Ave

New York Historical Society (E1, map 3 B3) Materials related to the history of New York and its people, including an unparalleled collection of artefacts related to September 11, 2001. • Tues, Wed, Thurs, Sat 10am–6pm, Fri 10am–8pm, Sun 11am–5.45pm ☎ 1 212 873-3400 • 170 Central Park West at 76th St ⑤ B, C: 81st St. Bus M10: 77th St, M79: 81st St

Children's Museum of Manhattan (map 3 B3) This is as much a play space as a museum, filled with hands-on exhibits where even the youngest kids can discover and explore science, the arts and the fascinating world around them. • Tues–Sun 10am–5pm ☎ 1 212 721-1234 • 212 W 83rd St near Broadway ⑤ 1: 86th St; B, C: 81st St. Bus M7, M10, M11, M104: W 83rd St

Riverside Park (C1, map 3 A1–3) The park stretches four miles along the western shore of Manhattan. Facilities include sports courts and fields, bike trail, skate park, kayak rental, cafe and, at 79th St, a marina that allows visitors direct access to Grant's Tomb (at 122nd St), the final resting place of Ulysses S. Grant, the Civil War hero and 18th president of the United States. • 72nd to 158th St along the Hudson River ⑤ 1, 2, 3: 72nd/96th Sts

Morningside Heights (map 4 K1) Just south of Harlem, this is the city's "student quarter," home of prestigious Columbia University, Barnard College, and numerous other academic institutions. Students and professors pop in and out of the area's many bookstores and inexpensive cafes. You'll recognize Tom's Restaurant at Broadway and W 112th St from the opening scenes of *Seinfeld*. • Bounded by 125th St, Morningside Park, 106th St and the Hudson River. ⑤ 1: 110th/116th Sts

Cathedral of St John the Divine (map 4 K1) Construction began in 1892, and it's still not finished. The fact that it's almost a century behind schedule seems to add to the legend of this massive building, which, one day, will be the world's largest neo-Gothic cathedral. The limestone and granite structure requires skilled stonemasons, who are being assisted by youngsters from Harlem. In the gift shop you can see a scale model of the cathedral as the architect must have imagined it. • Mon–Sat 7am–6pm; Sun 7am–7pm ☎ 1 212 316-7490 • 1047 Amsterdam Ave at 112th St ⑤ 1: 110th St

Harlem (map 4 K1) Harlem is one of the best-known black communities in America. During the first half of the 20th century, the residents established and popularized black arts, music and literature, with such famous names as James Baldwin, Paul Robeson, Langston Hughes, Louis Armstrong, Charlie Parker, Duke Ellington, Billie Holiday, Thelonius Monk and Dizzy Gillespie either living or performing here. This was also a political center, home to Marcus Garvey, Malcom X and W.E.B. DuBois. By mid-century, the neighborhood had declined as poverty, drug abuse and crime soared. Today, Harlem is back on its feet: several museums have opened; 125th St—the major commercial area—is filling with upscale stores; the Apollo Theater (253 W 125th St) has been renovated; many of the elegant brownstones have been refurbished and new luxury apartment buildings have opened. Don't miss Audubon Terrace on Broadway between 155th and 156th Sts, created as a modern-day acropolis, Sugar Hill, 155th to 145th St along Amsterdam Ave, once the country's most fashionable address for African Americans, and Striver's Row on W 138th and 139th Sts, between 7th and 8th Aves. • **Reaching north and east to the Harlem River, south to 110th St and west to Morningside and St Nicholas Aves** 🚇 A, C, 2, 3, 4, 5, 6: 125th St

Studio Museum in Harlem (map 4 K1) Founded in 1968 as a studio space for experimental art and artists, the Studio Museum boasts an impressive collection of paintings, sculptures and photographs by black artists from around the world. Before you leave, be sure to have a look at the publications and the stunning glass-bead jewellery in the gift shop. • Wed–Fri, Sun noon–6pm, Sat 10am–6pm ☎ 1 212 864-4500 • 144 W 125th St near Lenox Ave Ⓢ 2, 3, 4, 5, 6, A, B, C, D: 125th St

Abyssinian Baptist Church (map 4 L1) Known for its rousing gospel choir, this 1923 neo-Gothic church was home base for many years to Adam Clayton Powell, a preacher and congressman who was the most powerful man in Harlem. Try attending Sunday services at 9 or 11am. For groups of five or more, reservations are required at least two weeks in advance. ☎ 1 212 862-7474 ext 212 • 132 Odell Clark Place (138th St between Adam Clayton Powell and Malcolm X Blvds) Ⓢ 1: 137th St

Cloisters (off map 4 by L1) Devoted to medieval European art and architecture, the Cloisters is an enchanting place to visit. On a bluff overlooking the Hudson River, the museum incorporates sections of five French and Spanish medieval monasteries, a Romanesque chapel and a 12th-century Spanish apse. Among the exhibits are late-medieval tapestries depicting a unicorn hunt, a 12th-century Romanesque cross with over 100 carved figures, endless panes of stained-glass and rare illuminated manuscripts dating back almost 800 years. The courtyard gardens and view should not be missed. • March–Oct Tues–Sun 9.30am–5.15pm; Nov–Feb Tues–Sun 9.30am–4.45pm ☎ 1 212 923-3700 • Fort Tryon Park Ⓢ A to 190th St/ Washington Ave. Bus M4: Cloisters

Audubon Terrace (map 4 L1) This stunning museum complex is one of the city's best-kept secrets. Located on the hill that once held a farm owned by naturalist John James Audubon, Audubon Terrace was created by railroad heir Archer Huntington as a modern-day acropolis, a center of art and culture. Designed by leading architects of the day, including Stanford White and Cass Gilbert, it includes a Beaux-Arts plaza and buildings that house the Hispanic Society of America, the American Academy of Arts and Letters and Boricua College. • Broadway and W 155th St Ⓢ 1: 157th St. Bus M4, M5: 155th St

WALKING TOUR: MUSEUM MILE

Start with the largest, the **Metropolitan Museum of Art**, at 82nd St. The original Victorian Gothic design of this massive structure, opened in 1874, long ago vanished under a never-ending series of additions and updates. Hundreds of galleries contain over 2 million objects, but if you see only one thing, make it the superb collection of Egyptian Art.

The former Vanderbilt mansion on the corner of 86th St is the home of the **Neue Galerie**. Opened in 2001, this small-scale museum is devoted to early 20th century German and Austrian art and design and contains notable paintings by Gustav Klimt, Oskar Kokoschka, and Egon Schiele. Two blocks north, at 88th St, stands the **Solomon R. Guggenheim Museum**, where Frank Lloyd Wright's half-century old twisting and tilting design still stuns visitors. Take the elevator to the top and work your way down through the spiraling interior.

The **National Academy Museum and School of Fine Arts** at 89th Street offers a fine selection of 19th- and 20th-century American art in an intimate setting.

Cooper-Hewitt National Museum of Design at 91st Street is the only museum in the nation devoted exclusively to historic and contemporary design. In 1901, when industrialist Andrew Carnegie built this as his residence, he included every modern convenience; this was the first home in New York with a structural steel frame, passenger elevator, central heating and a precursor to air-conditioning.

One block north, the **Jewish Museum** at 92nd St explores 4,000 years of art and Jewish culture. Its collections range from archaeological artifacts to multi-media installations and films and there is a kosher café on the lower level.

Continue up 5th Avenue, into Spanish Harlem, for the **Museum of the City of New York** at 103rd St. Behind its block-long Georgian-Colonial brick façade rest 1.5 million objects and images related to the city, from its Dutch beginnings to the latest developments.

Across the street is Central Park's lovely **Conservatory Garden**, the only formal garden in the park. If you peek in on a summer weekend, you will surely catch a glimpse of at least one wedding party.

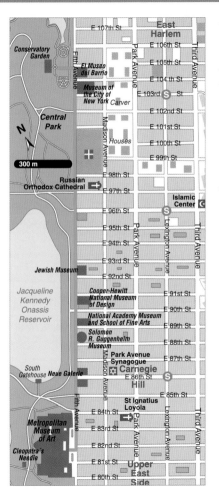

Some of the world's finest art institutions are only steps apart on a mile-long stretch of Fifth Avenue.

Start:
82nd St and Fifth Ave

Finish:
104th St and Fifth Ave

OUTER BOROUGHS

With all of Manhattan vying for your attention, it's easy to forget the city's four outlying boroughs: the Bronx, Queens, Brooklyn and Staten Island. But you'd be missing out if you stayed exclusively in Manhattan during your trip.

THE DISTRICTS AT A GLANCE

THE BRONX

The northernmost part of New York includes some of the city's most prosperous and impoverished areas. Although the Bronx boasts more parkland than any other borough, almost a quarter of the total area, much of the often gritty birthplace of rap, hip-hop and breakdancing is not yet tourist-friendly. Guided tours are available; see, for example, Susansez NYC Walkabouts, ☎ 917 509-3111

New York Botanical Gardens (map 4 L1) One of the few "true escapes" in the city, the gardens are home to the largest surviving stand of virgin forest

Cherry Blossom time draws the crowds to Prospect Park in Brooklyn.

that, centuries ago, covered all of New York City. The 100-ha (250-acre) park also boasts walking paths, an arboretum, a herbarium (with some 6 million specimens of dried plants), a rose garden, a world-class conservatory, a picnic area and two casual dining facilities. • Tues–Sun 10am–6pm; closed on certain holidays ☎1 718 817-8700 • Bronx River Parkway at Fordham Road ⑤ North Harlem line (from Grand Central Terminal): Botanical Gardens

Bronx Zoo (map 4 L1) The biggest zoo in the country featuring more than 6,000 animals of over 600 species that socialize, sleep and eat in "natural habitats". Highlights include the Tiger Mountain, JungleWorld, World of Birds, and a 6.5-acre Congo Gorilla Forest. • Apr–Oct Mon–Fri 10am–5pm, weekends and holidays to 5.30pm; Nov–Mar daily 10am–4.30pm ☎1 718 367-1010 • 2300 Southern Boulevard ⑤ 2, 5 to E Tremont Ave/ W Farm Square. Bus: BxM11: Bronx Zoo

THE SEXY SIDE OF THE CITY

When you are ready for some adult entertainment, New York is ready to supply it—with an attitude. Owned and managed by women, **Babeland** offers funky and fun toys, videos and accessories in a friendly atmosphere (94 Rivington St ☎ 1 212 375-1701; 43 Mercer St; 462 Bergen St, Brooklyn). If your taste and budget leans more towards silver and gold than plastic and rubber, head to **Myla** (20 E 69th St ☎ 1 212 570 1590) and **Kiki de Montparnasse** at 79 Greene St, by Spring St. Both offer luxurious lingerie and accessories for well-heeled connoisseurs.

Burlesque has made a comeback in the city. Combining glamour, dance, acrobatics and more than a touch of humour, these shows attract equal numbers of male and female fans. Be sure to see the critically acclaimed show at **Corio** on Thursday, Friday, and Saturday nights (337 West Broadway at Grand St ☎ 1 212 966-3901). If you visit in September, plan to attend the multi-day annual New York Burlesque Festival. For information, go to www.thenewyorkburlesquefestival.com.

For a more scholarly view, try the **Museum of Sex** dedicated to the uncensored exploration of human sexuality. Its collection contains over 15,000 items, including films, photos, magazines, costumes and paraphernalia from a wide range of cultures, countries and time periods (233 Fifth Ave at 23rd St ☎ 1 212 689-6337).

Rival downtown restaurants **Lucky Cheng's** (24 1st Ave at 1st St ☎ 1 212 995-5500) and **Lips** (2 Bank St at Greenwich Ave ☎ 1 212 675-7710) offer drag dining combined with raucous entertainment. Lucky Cheng's has a pan-Asian menu and the décor resembles a kitschy geisha house, while Lips serves an Italian-inspired menu. At both places, the main attraction is the performing waiters and bartenders, dressed in outrageous, fabulous fashions, who dish out the food and wisecracks with flair.

QUEENS

This is the largest and most diverse borough in the city, the size of Manhattan, the Bronx and Staten Island combined. A stunning 36 per cent of Queens residents are foreign-born. Koreans, Chinese, Greeks, Indians and Columbians have founded distinct ethnic communities here. Queens is largely residential, and has been spared much of the traffic congestion, noise, and over-development of Manhattan and other boroughs.

Isamu Noguchi Garden Museum (map 4 L2) A comprehensive collection of works by the Japanese-American sculptor (1904–1988) in stone, metal, wood, as well as clay and Akari Light Sculptures. • **Closed Mon and Tues** ☎ 1 718 204-7088 • 9-01 33rd Road between Vernon Boulevard and 10th St Ⓢ N, W: Broadway (Queens)

Museum of the Moving Image (map 4 L2) Closed for expansion; the museum is scheduled to re-open in winter 2009–10. ☎ 1 718 784-4520 www.movingimage.us • 35th Ave at 36th St

Queens Museum of Art (map 4 M2) The building dates back to the New York World's Fair of 1939 and houses a fantastic scale panorama showing the city in minute detail. • Wed–Fri 10am–5pm, Sat, Sun noon–5pm ☎ 1 718 592-9700 • Flushing Meadows Park Ⓢ 7 to Flushing then a 10-min walk. Bus Q48: Roosevelt Ave and 111th; Q23, Q58: Corona Ave and 51st Ave

BROOKLYN

With more residents (almost 2.5 million) than any other of New York's boroughs, an area of 210 sq km (80 sq miles), its own bustling business district, baseball team, beautiful parks and world-famous museums, Brooklyn is a city unto itself. Until 1898, it was entirely independent of New York City. Today, the borough that sits just across the East River—particularly Brooklyn Heights and Park Slope—continues to attract Manhattan residents: the rents are less expensive, the streets quieter and the atmosphere more bohemian. Brooklyn is also quite accessible to tourists, a 10-minute subway ride from Manhattan or a 20-minute stroll across Brooklyn Bridge.

Brooklyn Museum (map 4 K3) This is the city's second-largest art museum; its Egyptian, African and pre-Columbian art collections are world-renowned. While here, don't miss Judy *Chicago's Dinner Party* in the Elizabeth A. Sackler Center for Feminist Art. • Wed–Fri 10am–5pm Sat, Sun 11am–6pm (closes at 11 pm on the first Sat of each month) ☎ 1 718 638-5000 • 200 Eastern Parkway Ⓢ 2, 3: Eastern Parkway/Brooklyn Museum

Brooklyn Botanic Garden (map 4 K3) Highlights include the Japanese Garden, Rose Garden (with 1,200 varieties), Fragrance Garden (specially designed for the sight-impaired), Shakespeare Garden (flowers featured in the Bard's plays), and greenhouses. • Early March–Oct Tues–Fri 8am–6pm, Sat, Sun, holidays 10am–6pm; Nov–early Mar Tues–Fri 8am– 4.30pm, Sat, Sun, holidays 10am–4.30pm ☎ 1 718 623-7200 • 1000 Washington Ave at Eastern Parkway Ⓢ 2, 3: Eastern Parkway; B, Q: Prospect Park

Prospect Park (map 4 K3) The 213-ha park is a quiet, green oasis in urban Brooklyn. Its biggest attractions include a carousel, picnic areas, running paths, baseball diamonds, skating rink, a nature centre, an old Quaker cemetery where actor Montgomery Clift is buried, and a bandshell where concerts and dances are held during the summer. Recent performers include Lou Reed, Angelique Kidjo and Isaac Hayes. ☎ 1 718 965-8951 • Grand Army Plaza and Prospect Park West Ⓢ 2, 3: Grand Army Plaza; B, Q: Prospect Park

Prospect Park Zoo (map 4 K3) Just the right size for a delightful visit with red pandas, kangaroos, porcupines and 400 other animals of more than 80 species. Highlights include the sea-lion pool and discovery trail. • Apr–Oct Mon–Fri 10am–5pm, Sat, Sun 10am–5.30pm; Nov–Mar daily 10am–4.30pm ☎ 1 718 399-7339 • Flatbush Avenue Ⓢ B, Q: Prospect Park

Verrazano-Narrows Bridge (map 4 J4) With a 1,298-m (4,260-ft) span linking Brooklyn to Staten

Island, this was the world's longest suspension bridge when it was completed in 1964. Named after Italian explorer Giovanni da Verrazano, who sailed into New York Harbor in 1524.

STATEN ISLAND
Close to 450,000 predominantly white and middle-class New Yorkers live here. A free ferry carries commuters and tourists to and from the island, offering one of the best views of the Statue of Liberty and the New York skyline.

Historic Richmond Town (map 4 J4) Village and museum complex comprising 27 original buildings, the oldest being the Voorlezer House, c. 1695. • Hours vary; call ahead ☏ 1 718 351-1611 • 441 Clarke Ave. Bus S74 from ferry to Richmond Road and St Patrick's Place (40 min)

Jacques Marchais Museum of Tibetan Art (map 4 I4) The authentic replica of a Himalayan monastery with Tibetan artefacts. • Wed–Sun 1–5pm ☏ 1 718 987-3500 • 338 Lighthouse Ave. Bus S74 from ferry to Lighthouse Ave, walk up hill (10 min)

Alice Austen House Museum and Garden (map 4 J4) Austen (1866–1953) was one of the first American women to take up photography. Her house, Clear Comfort, built in 1690, is a museum of Victorian lifestyle. • Thurs–Sun noon–5pm. Closed Jan and Feb ☏ 1 718 816-4506 • 2 Hylan Blvd. Bus S51 from ferry to Hylan Blvd

Staten Island Museum (map 4 J3) American, European and Asian furniture and decorative arts. Also offers interactive children's programmes. • Mon–Sat 9am–5pm, Sun 1pm–5pm ☏ 1 718 727-1135 • 75 Stuyvesant Place, across from the ferry terminal

Staten Island September 11 Memorial (map 4 J3) When you leave the ferry, walk along the esplanade adjacent to the terminal to view the memorial. Its wing-like engraved twin "postcards" honor the 270 Staten Island residents who lost their lives during the 2001 attacks on the World Trade Center. • **North Shore Waterfront Esplanade**

WALKING TOUR: BROOKLYN HEIGHTS

Exit the subway at **Borough Hall**. Cross Court Street at Joralemon and head straight towards Clinton Street. The Tudor Gothic-style cluster of buildings on your left is **Packer Collegiate Institute**, an elite private school built in the 1850s. Turn right on Clinton and walk to Montague. On the northeast corner is the former Brooklyn Trust Company building (now **Chase Bank**), modeled after an Italian Renaissance palazzo. Duck inside to see the coffered ceiling and fine cosmatesque floor. Across Clinton, on the northwest corner, is **St Ann and the Holy Trinity Episcopal Church**. This brownstone gothic revival contains a magnificent pipe organ and is considered architect Minard Lafever's masterpiece. Turn left onto Montague; the tree-lined street is crowded with tempting shops, salons and cafes. **The Bossert**, at No. 98, was once one of the finest hotels in the city. Today it serves as a residence for Jehovah's Witnesses, whose world headquarters is nearby. Montague Street ends at the entrance to the **Brooklyn Heights Promenade**. This lovely area commands stunning views of Manhattan, the East River, the Brooklyn Bridge to the right and the Statue of Liberty to the left. Turn right onto the Promenade. Bronze plaques set into the slate walkway commemorate the view before and after 9/11. Walk to the right and exit the Promenade at Clark Street. Go straight, and then turn left onto **Willow Street**. No. 70, built in the 1830s, was home to prominent 20th-century authors and musicians including W.H. Auden, Benjamin Britten, Christopher Isherwood, Carson McCullers and Truman Capote, who immortalized it in his book, *A House on the Heights*. Turn right onto Orange Street. At the corner of Hicks Street is the **Plymouth Church of the Pilgrims**. In 1849, when it was built, the church was led by Rev. Henry Ward Beecher, America's most famous abolitionist. Go inside for a good view of the stained-glass windows made by Louis Comfort Tiffany; the basement was a stop on the Underground Railroad and used to shelter runaway slaves.

Exiting the church, make a right and proceed to Middagh Street. Turn left to see No. 24, an old wooden Federal-style house built in 1824. Walk back up Middagh to Cadman Plaza. Go through the park, where signs lead to the **Brooklyn Bridge**. Strolling across, especially at dusk, you'll see all Manhattan spread out at your feet like a huge welcome mat.

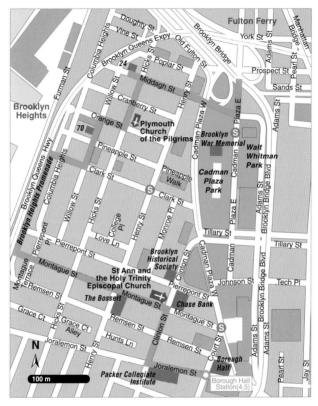

A CHARMING TASTE OF OLD NEW YORK IN THE BOROUGH OF CHURCHES

Located on a bluff high above the East River, Brooklyn Heights was the first section of the city to be designated a historic district, enabling the neighborhood to retain much of its 19th century scale and charm.

Start: Borough Hall **Finish:** Brooklyn Bridge

RIDE THE INTERNATIONAL EXPRESS

To see a side of the city rarely glimpsed by tourists, take a ride on the International Express, the nickname given to the #7 local subway. The train's 7-mile route, which has been honored as a National Millennium Trail, takes you from Times Square to Flushing, Queens. Along the way you'll pass through a series of immigrant neighborhoods. This is the most ethnically diverse area in the world populated by people from 150 nations.

During much of the trip, the train will travel at—or above—ground level. As you approach Vernon Boulevard-Jackson Avenue at **Long Island City**, the first station in Queens, you'll see a large building covered entirely in bright paint. That is **5-Pointz**, a former warehouse now legally used as a canvas by graffiti writers who make pilgrimages here from around the world.

The **Woodside** neighborhood, once known as Irishtown, has long been a centre of Irish-American life. Hop off here and you'll find pubs pouring Guinness and delis selling Irish newspapers. The **Starting Gate Pub** has live music on weekends and shows all GAA (Gaelic) football matches (59-10 Woodside Ave).

Jackson Heights is home to vibrant South Asian and Latino communities. While India, Pakistan and Bangladesh don't always happily co-exist back home, their citizens live side by side in Queens. This is the place to watch a Bollywood movie, get a henna tattoo or pick up a packet of incense. Don't miss local

favourites the **India Sari Palace**, known for its jewel-toned silk fabrics (37-07 74th St) or the **Jackson Diner** with an enormously popular all-you-can-eat lunch buffet (37-47 74th St).

Nearby, Spanish is the primary language spoken. The residents in this section of Jackson Heights hail from Mexico, South and Central America and the Caribbean, and in warm weather Roosevelt Avenue is lined with vendors selling fresh sweet and savoury treats. **Zapateria Mexico** is where many of New York's mariachi bands buy their sombreros (88-07 Roosevelt Ave).

Corona has a thriving Muslim community, with many residents that hail from the Middle East, Africa and South Asia. There are halal butcher shops, religious book vendors and a large mosque, the **Masjid Alfalah House of Worship** where the faithful gather to pray five times a day (42-12 National Ave).

The final stop on the #7 is in **Flushing**, New York's largest Chinatown. This area also contains the city's largest Korean population. Walk out of the station and you will be surrounded by herb shops, fish markets and bakeries, all their fragrances mingling. Be sure to visit **Ten Ren Tea & Ginseng**, a branch of Taiwan's leading tea company (135-18 Roosevelt Ave) as well as **Corner 28** (40-28 Main St) where you can buy a Peking Duck bun for less than $1.

cityBites

The first real restaurant in the US appeared in 1830, when two Swiss brothers set up a European-style establishment where local businessmen could come for meals—the legendary Delmonico's. Today there are 10,000 restaurants in New York City. Some of the more expensive establishments require reservations, so it's best to phone ahead and check. And remember this simple trick when you're figuring out the tip, which is never included in the bill: just double the tax.

We have included cafés and coffeehouses in this section for those who just want a quick snack or respite from shopping or sightseeing. Each of the restaurants is coded to give an approximate idea of the price per person for a meal. The categories are:

1	below $16
2	$17–$30
3	$31–$50
4	$50 or more

Gigino

Bamn!

FINANCIAL DISTRICT

Bridge Café
🟢 2, 3: Fulton St;
4, 5, 6: City Hall/
Brooklyn Bridge
279 Water St at Dover St
☎ 1 212 227-3344
3

Next to the Brooklyn
Bridge, this is the oldest
surviving tavern in New
York, located in a wooden
building erected in 1794.

City Hall
🟢 1, 2, 3, A, C:
Chambers St
131 Duane St (between
Church and W Broaway)
☎ 1 212 227-7777
3

Spacious, elegant
American brasserie, with
great photos of old New
York on the walls and
good food.

Delmonico's
🟢 2, 3: Wall St;
4, 5: Bowling Green;
R, W: Whitehall St
56 Beaver St, near
William St
☎ 212 509-1144
4

The first restaurant in
America, this classic
steakhouse (birthplace of
Eggs Benedict and
Lobster Newburg) has
been a favourite of Wall
Streeters since 1837.

Gigino at Wagner Park
🟢 1: Rector St; 4, 5:
Bowling Green
20 Battery Place
(West St)
☎ 1 212 528-2228
3

Harbour view including
the Statue of Liberty, lots
of atmosphere at this
Italian trattoria.

Kitchenette
🟢 1, 2, 3, A, C:
Chambers St
156 Chambers St at
W Broadway
☎ 1 212 267-6740
2

Friendly spot beloved for
home-style breakfasts and
baked goods. Don't miss
the pies.

DOWNTOWN

Angelica Kitchen
🟢 L: 1st/3rd Ave
300 E 12th St between
1st and 2nd Ave
☎ 1 212 228-2909
2

Legendary organic
vegan cooking in the East
Village.

Baluchi's
🟢 C, E: Spring St
193 Spring St, between

Sullivan and Thompson
(one of 12 locations)
☎ 1 212 226-2828
2
City-wide chain offering
Indian fare specially
tailored for American
palates.

Bamn!
$ 6: Astor Place
37 St Mark's Place at
2nd Ave

☎ 1 888 400-2266
1
Hipsters flock to this
colourful, casual spot
where cheap fast food is
sold from machines until
late into the night.

Bar 89
$ 6, C, E: Spring St;
N, R: Prince St
89 Mercer St between
Broome and Spring Sts

☎ 1 212 274-0989
2
If there exists such a thing
as a chic salad, you'll find
it here. And upstairs are
the most spectacular WCs
on the East Coast.

Bolo
$ N, R, W: 23rd St
23 E 22nd St

JEWISH-STYLE CUISINE

Large numbers of
Eastern European
Jews moved to New
York at the turn of the
20th century and soon
popularized their
hearty, homey style of
cooking.
The delis and
restaurants listed
below feature the
city's best traditional
Jewish-style takeaway
and sit-down meals.
B&H Dairy
$ 6: Astor Place
127 2nd Ave near St
Mark's Place
Carnegie Deli
$ N, R: 57th St
854 7th Ave at 55th St
Ess-a-Bagel
$ 6: 23rd St
359 1st Ave at 21st St,

Also at 831 3rd Ave
near 50th St
H&H Bagels West
$ 1: 79th St
2239 Broadway at
80th St. Open 24h
Katz's Deli
$ F, V: 2nd Ave
205 East Houston
St at Ludlow St.
Kossar's Bialys
$ F: Delancey
137 Grand Street at
Essex
*Stammy's Roumanian
Steak House*
$ J, M, Z: Bowery;
F, V: 2nd Ave
157 Chrystie St near
Delancey St
Second Avenue Deli
$ 6: 33rd St
162 E 33rd St near 3rd
Ave

☎ 1 212 228-2200
3

More Art Deco than Madrid inside, but it's a top contender for the city's best Spanish food—hearty, colourful and inspired.

Caffè Reggio
⑤ A, B, C, D, E, F, V: W 4th St/ Washington Sq
119 MacDougal St, between Minetta Lane and W 3rd Sts
☎ 1 212 475-9557
This is the oldest coffee-house in Greenwich Village. Great espresso, great people-watching.

Caffè Taci
⑤ 6: Astor Place; N, R, W: 8th St
10 Waverly Place at Mercer St
☎ 1 212 473-3944
3

Decent Italian food. Known for its "opera nights" every Friday and Saturday, when professionals and patrons alike take to the stage. Dinner $30 minimum per person, bar $15 minimum.

Country Café
⑤ C, E: Spring St
69 Thompson St, between Broome and Spring Sts
☎ 1 212 966-5417
2

Either Moroccan cuisine with a heavy French influence, or the other way around. In any case, it's a gem of a restaurant.

Cupping Room Café
⑤ C, E: Spring St
359 West Broadway at Broome St
☎ 1 212 925-2898
2

The perfect spot for a brunch or just a snack. An omelette, a coffee, and off you go to tour SoHo.

El Faro
⑤ A, C, E, L: 14th St
823 Greenwich St at Horatio
☎ 1 212 929-8210
2

Well-prepared Spanish cuisine. Start with the sangria, following up with the paella, ribs or shrimp *ajillo*.

Golden Unicorn
⑤ J, M, N, Q, R, W, 6: Canal St;
B, D: Grand St
18 E Broadway at Catherine St
3rd Floor
☎ 1 212 941-0911
2

This is a great spot for a dim-sum Sunday brunch, but be sure to get there early. Take the lift to the third floor and, behold, you have found your way

to Chinese dumpling heaven.

Gotham Bar & Grill
⑤ N, R, Q, W, 4, 5, 6: 14th St/Union Square
12 E 12th St
☎ 1 212 620-4020
4

Fine New American cuisine. Popular, pricey spot consistently voted one of the city's best.

HanGawi
⑤ 6: 33rd St; B, D, F, N, Q, R, V, W: 34th St
12 E 32nd St
☎ 1 212 213-0077
3

Fine Korean vegetarian restaurant in the heart of "Koreatown." Pillows double as seats, and you have to remove your shoes.

Joe's Shanghai
⑤ 6, J, M, Q, R, W: Canal St
9 Pell St between Bow-ery and Mott Sts (one of three locations)
☎ 1 212 233-8888
3

Go here for their famous soup dumplings. Usually crowded.

Kang Suh Restaurant
⑤ B, D, F, N, R, V, W: 34th St
1250 Broadway at 32nd St

☎ 1 212 564-6845
2

Tender marinated raw meats and seafood make for a sumptuous grill-it-yourself meal.

Kin Khao
🟢 C, E: Spring St
171 Spring St (between Thompson and West Broadway)
☎ 1 212 966-3939
2

The queue can be a bit long for dinner, but it's well worth the wait. Excellent Thai curries and other spicy dishes with coconut milk, prepared in full view. Loud, boisterous atmosphere.

Knickerbocker Bar & Grill
🟢 R, W: 8th St;
6: Astor Place
33 University Place and 9th St
☎ 1 212 228-8490
3

Classic steak and potatoes spot in Greenwich Village. They often host jazz bands at dinnertime.

Lombardi's
🟢 6: Spring St
32 Spring St
between Mott and Mulberry Sts
☎ 1 212 941-7994
1

Union Square Café

Legendary. Open since 1905, the first pizzeria in the US. Don't miss their inimitable clam pizza.

Moustache Pitza
🟢 1: Christopher St/ Sheridan Square
90 Bedford St, between Barrow and Grove Sts
☎ 1 212 229-2220
1

Middle Eastern restaurant, prized for fragrant, crispy "pitzas".

The Odeon
🟢 1, 2, 3: Chambers St
145 West Broadway at Duane St
☎ 1 212 233-0507
3

Legendary TriBeCa hot spot that is still "in". Good American-French fare. Best late night, when the arty crowd shows up.

One if By Land, Two if By Sea
🟢 A, B, C, D, E, F, V: W 4th St
17 Barrow St at 7th Ave S
☎ 1 212 228-0822
3

Famed as the most romantic restaurant in the city. Live piano music, classic French and American dishes by firelight.

Peanut Butter & Co
🟢 A, C, E, F: W 4th St
240 Sullivan St at Bleecker St
☎ 1 212 677-3995
1

A cosy kitchen-like setting for this place offering everything from sandwiches to sweets made with peanut butter that is freshly ground on the premises.

Union Square Cafe
🚇 L, N, R, 4, 5, 6:
14th St/Union Square
21 E 16th St
☎ 1 212 243-4020
3

Local food critics can't praise this place enough. The New American cuisine is exemplary, the atmosphere classy, the service perfect.

MIDTOWN

Aquavit
🚇 6: Lexington Ave/51st St; E, V: 53rd St/5th Ave
65 E 55th St near Madison
☎ 1 212 307-7311
4

Ethiopian-born chef Marcus Samuelsson serves traditional Scandinavian delicacies, and innovative aquavits.

Barbetta
🚇 1, 2, 3, 7, A, C, E, N, R, S, Q, W: Times Square/42nd St
321 W 46th St
☎ 1 212 246-9171
4

Some of the best Italian food in the city. The garden is a perfect spot for pre-theatre dinner.

Café Centro
🚇 4, 5, 6, N, R: Grand Central Terminal;
S from Times Square

Café Centro

200 Park Ave, between 45th St and Vanderbilt Ave
☎ 1 212 818-1222
3

French-Mediterranean brasserie next to Grand Central Terminal.

Four Seasons
🚇 6: 51st, E, V: 53rd St
99 E 52nd St
☎ 1 212 754-9494
4

A New York institution, catering to the rich and famous. Classic American and international cuisine. Business attire required, reservations essential.

Gilt at The New York Palace Hotel
🚇 B, D, F, Q, V: 47th–50th Sts/Rockefeller Center; E: 53rd St;
6: 51st St

455 Madison Ave
☎ (212) 891 8100
4

Located in the hotel's 1882 Villard Mansion, this sleek new restaurant combines an opulent décor with an innovative cuisine that changes with the seasons. Grand menus of three, five or seven courses, attentive waiters and fine wines from the extensive wine list.

Hard Rock Cafe
🚇 1, 2, 3, 7, A, C, E, N, Q, R, S, W: Times Square/42nd St
1501 Broadway
☎ 1 212 343-3355
3

The queues are long, the place is teeming with tourists, the food ("casual American fare") is mediocre, but people

Smith & Wollensky

seem to put up with it just to say they went to the Hard Rock Cafe.

Rainbow Room
🚇 B, D, F, V: 47th–50th Sts/Rockefeller Center
30 Rockefeller Plaza, 65th Floor
☎ 1 212 632-5100
4

A romantic, elegant venue for an extra-special night out. The food is exquisite, the view is inspiring and you'll feel like a star.

Rock Center Café
🚇 B, D, F, V: 47th–50th Sts/Rockefeller Center
Rockefeller Center, Skating Rink
20 W 50th St
☎ 1 212 332-7620
3

During the Christmas season, you'll have a cheery view of the ice skaters and Christmas tree; in summer the tables and bar move outside. The Italian-accented food plays second fiddle to the view.

Russian Samovar
🚇 1, C, E: 50th St
256 W 52nd St (between Broadway and 8th Ave)
☎ 1 212 757-0168
3

Featured in *Sex and the City*, this is a pleasant spot for vodka and stroganoff.

Smith & Wollensky
🚇 6: 51st St,
E, V: Lexington Ave/ 53rd St

797 3rd Ave at 49th St
☎ 1 212 753-1530
4

A New York institution famous for its porterhouse steaks, fresh seafood, lobster, wines and after-dinner cigars, all in an elegant setting.

Tamarind
🚇 6: 23rd St
41–43 E 22nd St at Broadway
☎ 1 212 674-7400
3

First-rate Indian food served with care in a delectable setting. Don't miss the saffron-laced she-crab soup and the tender tandooris.

Zarela

Le Bilboquet

Zarela
S 6, E, V: 51st St
953 2nd Ave,
between 50th and
51st Sts
☎ 1 212 644-6740
2

Top-rated Mexican eats
and the best margaritas in
town; this place is perfect
for lunch after a tour of
the UN.

Zen Palate
S A, C, E: 8th Ave/
42nd St
663 9th Ave at 46th St
Also at 104 John St
(Financial District)
☎ 1 212 501-7768
2

This duo of Asian-
influenced restaurants
cooks up light and
extraordinarily flavourful
dishes. An essential stop
for vegetarians.

UPTOWN

Amy Ruth's
S 2, 3, B, C: 116th St
113 W 116th St at
7th Ave
☎ 1 212 280-8779
2

By far the best soul food
(ribs, fried chicken, fresh
vegetables) in the north-
east US.

Café des Artistes
S 1: 66th St;
B, C to 72nd St
1 W 67th St at Central
Park West
☎ 1 212 877-3500
4

French cuisine of the
highest order and a
romantic interior have
placed the Café des
Artistes at the summit
(the six murals depicting
wood nymphs are by

Howard Chandler Christy,
1873–1952). The steak
tartare and raw oysters
are delectable.

Café Con Leche
S 1: 79th St
424 Amsterdam Ave,
between 80th and
81st Sts
Also at 726 Amsterdam
Ave near 95th St
☎ 1 212 595-7000
2

Sumptuous Cuban food
that makes you want to
fly straight to Havana.

Cafe Luxembourg
S 1, 2, 3, B, C: 72nd St
200 W 70th St between
Amsterdam and
West End Aves
☎ 1 212 873-7411
3

Classic venue for French-
American fare. Flattering

lighting and unflappable staff. Good brunch on Saturdays and Sundays.

Carlyle Restaurant
S 6: 77th St
Carlyle Hotel
35 E 76th St
☎ 1 212 570-7192
4

Fortuny fabric-covered walls and engravings by Pierre-Joseph Redouté (1759–1840), classic French cuisine, impeccable service and sky-high prices.

Le Bilboquet
S 4, 5, 6: 59th; F: Lexington Ave/63rd St; N, R, W: 59th St/5th Ave
25 E 63rd St
☎ 1 212 751-3036
3

Small French restaurant on the Upper East Side.

The dishes are superb, the wine list excellent.

Tavern on the Green
S 1: 66th St
Central Park West and 67th St
☎ 1 212 873-3200
4

Over-the-top extravagance strictly for tourists; fabulous terrace in summer. The cooking takes a back seat to the décor and gift shop, but it's an experience, all the same.

BROOKLYN

Al Di La
S M, R: Union St
248 5th Ave (at Carroll St)
☎ 1 718 636-8888
3

No reservations. Delicious Venetian cooking at Brooklyn prices.

Applewood
S F: 7th Ave
501 11th St at 7th Ave
☎ 1 718 768-2044
2

Modern American cuisine with a cheerful emphasis on organic ingredients.

Peter Luger Steak House
S J, M, Z: Marcy Ave
Taxi recommended
178 Broadway
(Driggs Ave)
☎ 1 718 387-7400
4

One of the oldest and best steak houses in the country. No credit cards.

River Café
S A, C: High St; 2, 3: Clark St, or take a cab
1 Water St
☎ 1 71) 522-5200
4

American menu, priceless view of Manhattan. Fixed price only for dinner and Sunday brunch.

Saul
S F: Bergen St;
140 Smith St at Bergen St
☎ 1 718 935-9844
3

Sophisticated American food, low-key atmosphere at the heart of Brooklyn's restaurant row.

SATISFY YOUR SWEET TOOTH

After you've spent the day walking all over the city, your waistline can afford a bit of indulgence. Reward yourself with some of the sweetest treats in New York.

Midtown

Juniors: their legendary creamy cheesecake has been voted the best in the city year after year (W 45th near Broadway, ☎ 1 212 302-2000; Grand Central Terminal Dining Concourse; 386 Flatbush Ave, Brooklyn).

Apple pie is the classic American dessert, and **Little Pie Company** is famed for their Sour Cream Apple Walnut Pie, available in three sizes (424 W 43rd St between 9th and 10th Ave ☎ 1 212 736-4780; also Grand Central Terminal Dining Concourse). **Beard Papa**, a Japanese bakery, makes cream puffs that have a cult following. Pop these delectable treats into your mouth as soon as they are filled (18 E 41st St at 5th Ave ☎ 1 212 779-0600; also 740 Broadway; 2167 Broadway; 5 Carmine St).

Uptown

Owned by designer Ralph Lauren's daughter, **Dylan's Candy Bar** sells 5,000 types of candy and even has candy inlaid in the stairs (1011 Lexington Ave at 60th St ☎ 1 646 735-0078).

Simply the best: Junior's cheesecake.

Beard Papa's little cream puffs.

Grom is the first US branch of an Italian chain. The ingredients for their luscious *gelato* are grown and prepared in Italy, then shipped to NY where they are spun on-site (2165 Broadway at 76th St ☎ 212 362-1837; also 233 Bleecker St at Carmine).

A Harlem institution, **Make My Cake** is loved for its old-fashioned Southern-style baking. Their Red Velvet Cake is a neighbourhood favourite (121 St Nicholas Ave at 116th St ☎1 212-932-0833; 2380 Adam C. Powell Blvd at 139th St).

Downtown

At **Jacques Torres Chocolate Factory** you can watch confections being made while you sip the city's finest hot chocolate (350 Hudson at King St near Houston St ☎ 1 212 414-2462; 66 Water St, Brooklyn).

Rice to Riches sells rice pudding in a futuristic setting. Don't miss the lemon and mango flavours (37 Spring St near Mulberry St ☎ 1 212 274-0008).

Magnolia Bakery has been a phenomenon since it appeared on *Sex in the City*. Due to its popularity, purchases are limited to 12 cupcakes per customer (401 Bleecker St at W 11th St ☎ 1 212 462-

Eclairs with flair.

2572; 200 Columbus Ave at W 69th St).

A tiny restaurant serving only dessert, **ChikaLicious** has a 3-course *prix fixe* menu that changes daily. Go before 8pm to avoid the after-dinner crowds (203 E 10th Street, between 1st and 2nd Ave ☎ 1 212 995-9511).

Babycakes proves that healthy treats can also be delicious with their vegan, sugar- and wheat-free baked goods (248 Broome St near Ludlow ☎ 1 212 677-5047).

cityNights

Once the sun sets, New York becomes another creature altogether and your options multiply. You can see some world-class opera at Lincoln Center, catch a film at the venerable Ziegfeld Theater or hit a Broadway show. Have a drink at a downtown tavern or check out an up-and-coming punk band in the East Village. A good tip: keep an extra $20 on hand to take a taxi if you're out late. *New York Magazine, Time Out, The New York Times* and the "Voice Choice" section of *The Village Voice* all have detailed entertainment listings.

NO SMOKING!

Much of the city (at least, the interior spaces) is nearly smoke-free. While tobacco smoking is still legal in New York, the law makes it expensive and inconvenient. No one under 18 can buy cigarettes and the price is among the highest in the nation. One pack of 20 cigarettes is about $10, nearly twice as much they cost across the river in New Jersey. It is illegal to smoke in most public buildings and workplaces. If you want to light up in a store, taxi, bus, train, airport, museum, bar, restaurant or theatre, forget about it. Break the law and you could be fined up to $1,000. As a result, New Yorkers go outside into the streets to smoke. No matter what the weather, you'll generally find groups of smokers clustered around the entrances of buildings and indulging their habit.

BALLET, OPERA, CLASSICAL MUSIC

Most of the city's classical performances take place at Lincoln Center, a complex of several buildings on Broadway and 65th St. The New York State Theater (home to the NYC Ballet and the NYC Opera) is the southernmost building; the Metropolitan Opera House is in the centre, and Avery Fisher Hall to the north.
For tickets, call Centercharge at 1 212 721-6500 or Telecharge at 1 212 239-6200 or go directly to the box office.

American Ballet Theatre
🚇 1: 66th St
Lincoln Center
Metropolitan Opera House
☎ 1 212 447-3030
Since 1940, this dance company has enthralled audiences with classics like *Sleeping Beauty, La Bayadère* and *Swan Lake*. Nureyev, Mikhail Baryshnikov and Cynthia Gregory have all graced the stage.

Carnegie Hall
🚇 A, B, C, D, 1: Columbus Circle;
N, Q, R, W: 57th St
57th St and 7th Ave
☎ 1 212 247-7800
Carnegie Hall is best known for hosting world-famous orchestras, but jazz, folk and rock bands (notably the Beatles) have played here.

Metropolitan Opera House
🚇 1 to 66th St
Lincoln Center
☎ 1 212 362-6000
The Met attracts the brightest stars of the operatic heavens: Cecilia Bartoli, Placido Domingo and Kathleen Battle, among others.

New York City Ballet
🚇 1: 66th St
Lincoln Center
New York State Theater
☎ 1 212 870-5570
Another venerated city ballet company. George Balanchine's *The Nutcracker* is staged during the Christmas season.

New York City Opera
🚇 1: 66th St
Lincoln Center
New York State Theater
☎ 1 212 870-5570
Like the Met, the City Opera stages the classic operas, though it tackles more eclectic pieces as well.

New York Philharmonic
Ⓢ 1: 66th St
Lincoln Center
Avery Fisher Hall
☎ 1 212 875-5656
Directed by conductor Lorin Maazel since 2002, the Philharmonic satisfies the city's love for classical music, performing some 200 concerts per year.

BARS

ArtBar
Ⓢ A, C, E: 14th St
52 8th Ave
between Horatio and Jane Sts
☎ 1 212 727-0244
A West Village hangout, best in late afternoon. Cosy back room with low, comfy couches and dim lighting.

Bookmarks Bar at the Library Hotel
Ⓢ 4, 5, 6, 7, S: Grand Central Station/42nd St
299 Madison Ave at 41st St
☎ 1 212 983-4500
Sip your drinks by the fireside in this elegant wood-panelled bar, or sit out on the rooftop terrace to enjoy great views over the city. The terrace is glassed in and heated in winter. Avoid early evening and the after-work crowd.

Café Un Deux Trois
Ⓢ 1, 2, 3, 7, 9, N, R, S: 42nd St/Times Square
123 W 44th St
☎ 1 212 354-4148
A former hotel lobby catering to midtown residents and post-theatre crowds. There are crayons on every table so you can idle away the time by colouring the tablecloths.

Campbell Apartment
Ⓢ 4, 5, 6, 7, S: Grand Central/42nd St
Grand Central Terminal
15 Vanderbilt Ave near 43rd St
☎ 1 212 953-0409
Elegant lounge in the restored private offices of American railroad tycoon John W. Campbell.

Corner Bistro
Ⓢ A, C, E, L: 14th St
331 W 4th St at Jane St
☎ 1 212 242-9502
Fabulous hamburgers and chips, locally

THEATRE

Musicals and more established playwrights generally grab the stages on Broadway and the Times Square area, while avant-garde and up-and-coming shows are relegated to Off-Broadway and elsewhere in town. Discount tickets (up to 50% off) for many shows are available at TKTS in Times Square and at less crowded locations in Brooklyn and the Financial District. In order to receive the discount, you must buy tickets on the day of the performance.

brewed beer, a variety of choice Scotches and one of the best jukeboxes in the city.

Landmark Tavern
🚇 A, C, E: 42nd St
626 11th Ave at 46th St
☎ 1 212 247-2562
A bar that's been in the same location since 1868.

McSorley's Old Ale House
🚇 6: Astor Place;
N, R: 8th St
15 E 7th St
☎ 1 212 474-9148
Mugs of home-brewed ale served up here since 1854 in a fantastic old-tavern atmosphere.

Mona's
🚇 L: 1st Ave
224 Ave B, between 13th and 14th Sts
☎ 1 212 353-3780
Grungy, but offering a glimpse of old-fashioned East Village punk culture. There's no sign outside, but it's the only bar on the block.

Trailer Park Lounge & Grill
🚇 1, C, E: 23rd St
271 W 23rd St at 8th Ave
☎ 1 212 463-8000
As kitschy as they come, this place is modeled on a hillbilly trailer park. Traditional American specialities such as steak sandwiches, hamburgers, chili and nachos, and potent cocktails.

White Horse Tavern
🚇 1: Christopher St;
A, C, E: 14th St
567 Hudson St at 11th St
☎ 1 212 243-9260
Fabled West Village watering hole, where Dylan Thomas and friends drank themselves to death. Dark and crowded, serving students, locals and tourists.

CONTEMPORARY MUSIC

Arlene's Grocery
🚇 F, V: 2nd Ave;
J, M, Z: Essex St
95 Stanton St at Ludlow St
☎ 1 212 995-1652
A former Lower East Side food store known for supporting new and

emerging bands. Hear them here before they're famous.

Beauty Bar
🚇 4, 5, 6, N, R: Union Square; L: 3rd Ave
231 E 14th St at 2nd Ave
☎ 1 212 539-1389
A former beauty salon transformed into a glam saloon bar in 1995, complete with chrome-domed hair dryers. The only beauty treatment you'll get there nowadays is a manicure, served up with a cocktail.
Eclectic pop and rock music.

The Bitter End
🚇 A, B, C, D, E, F, V:
W 4th St
147 Bleecker St at LaGuardia Pl.
☎ 1 212-673-7030
The city's oldest rock club features new singer/song-writers, Bob Dylan, Norah Jones and Patti Smith are among those who got their start here.

Bowery Ballroom
⊖ F: 2nd Ave; J, M:
Bowery; B, D: Grand St
6 Delancey St, between
Bowery and Chrystie Sts
☎ 1 212 533-2111
It may sound tame but
this former vaudeville

theatre is the best venue
in New York for rock,
independent and under-
ground music. Courtney
Love, The White Stripes,
Coldplay and Interpol
have all performed here.
Excellent sound system.

The Living Room
⊖ F, V: Lower East
Side/2nd Ave;
F, J, M, Z: Delancey/
Essex
158 Ludlow St at
Rivington St
☎ 1 212 505-3733

OPEN 24 HOURS

There's a good reason
New York is called
"the city that never
sleeps"—in addition
to dozens of all-night
restaurants and
pharmacies, here are
some places you might
be surprised to find
open 24 hours a day.
James A. Farley Station,
the magnificent main
branch of the post
office, is always open
for buying stamps and
mailing packages (441
Eighth Ave between
31st and 33rd Sts).
*Graphics Service
Bureau*: on-demand
digital printing,
reproduction, binding
and document
imaging (370 Park
Avenue South at 26th
St, Mon–Fri 24 hours,
Sat 10am–6pm).

*Apple Store Fifth
Avenue*: buy an iPod,
obtain service or just
go online in this slick
temple of high tech
(767 5th Ave between
58th and 59th Sts).
HomeFront Hardware:
three floors packed
with hardware and
houseware, everything
from lumber to frying
pans (202 E 29th St
between 2nd and 3rd
Aves).

24-7 Fitness Club: a
serious gym with yoga
and boxing, you can
purchase a one-day
membership for $15
or one-month for $60
(47 W 14th St
between 5th and 6th
Aves).
Juvenex Spa: sauna,
massage, wraps, peels
and more (25 W 32nd
St, 5th Floor; women
only 7am–7pm, open
to all 7pm–7am).

A relaxed, unpretentious spot to catch the latest indie bands. Live shows performed seven nights a week.

Mercury Lounge
🚇 F, V: Lower East Side/2nd Ave
217 E Houston St at Essex St
☎ 1 212 260-4700
A real music lover's venue with one of the most mind-blowing sound systems in NYC. Up and coming rock bands.

Pete's Candy Store
🚇 G, L: Metropolitan Ave/Lorimer St
709 Lorimer St at Richardson St, Brooklyn
☎ 1 718 302-3770
Rated as one of the best bars in New York, this venue has three rooms—and a backyard for parties. Live music of all kinds, from folk to ska, nightly, as well as readings by literary icons, Quizz-Off nights, bingo and spelling bees.

JAZZ, BLUES AND CABARET

Bar Next Door
🚇 A, B, C, D, E, F, V: W 4th St
129 MacDougal St at 3rd St
☎ 1 212 529-5945

Located in a Village basement, featuring excellent jazz in a candlelit setting.

Birdland
🚇 A, C, E: 42nd St
315 W 44th St at 8th Ave
☎ 1 212 581-3080
Named after Charlie "Bird" Parker, this club has hosted the likes of Dizzy Gillespie and Count Basie in its day. It still attracts some of the best.

Blue Note
🚇 1: Christopher St; A, B, C, D, E, F, Q: W 4th St
131 W 3rd St
☎ 1 212 475-8592
The most venerated jazz club in the city. The cover charge is heavy, but expect to be blown away.

Cleopatra's Needle
🚇 1, 2, 3: 96th St
2485 Broadway at 92nd St
☎ 1 212 769-6969
Relaxed atmosphere in Cleo's, a venue near Central Park specializing in live jazz, with infinite jam sessions ending every evening. Good food (Mediterranean cuisine), drinks, as well as live sports coverage on a big TV screen. $10 minimum charge.

Don't Tell Mama
🚇 1, 2, 3, 7, A, C, E, N, Q, R, S, W: 42nd St/ Times Square
343 W 46th St at 9th Ave
☎ 1 212 757-0788
Small and intimate award-winning venue comprising piano bar (no reservations) and two cabaret rooms; drinks only. Shows vary from rock n'roll to comedy groups and female impersonators. Lots of good-humoured fun but nothing to make Mama blush.

Jazz Standard
🚇 6: 28th St
116 E 27th St, between Lexington and Park Aves
☎ 1 212 576-2232
Great music, intimate setting and excellent food provided by barbecue specialists.

Joe's Pub
🚇 R, W: 8th St; 6: Astor Place
425 Lafayette St at Astor Place
☎ 1 212 539-8777
Tickets: ☎ 1 212 967-7555 10am–9pm or on-line www.joespub.com; dinner reservations:
☎ 1 212 539-8778; seating and standing room on first-come first-served basis

Lush venue with candlelit atmosphere and velvet couches. Classic Italian dinner menu and speciality cocktails. Headliners have ranged from Amy Winehouse to Leonard Cohen.

Marie's Crisis
🄢 1: Christopher St/ Sheridan Square; A, B, C, D, E, F, V: W 4th St/Washington Square 59 Grove St at 7th Ave
☎ 1 212 243-9323
American revolutionary Thomas Paine died on this site in 1809; the current building (1839) is named for his *Crisis Papers*. In a dark downstairs room, this is an entertaining gay bar with sing-along showtunes, often with Broadway stars.

The Oak Room at the Algonquin Hotel
🄢 7, N, Q, R, S, W: Times Square; B, D, F, V: 42nd St 59 W 44th St at 5th Ave
☎ 1 212 840-6800
Sophisticated supper club. Cabaret artists who've played here include Harry Connick Jr., Michael Feinstein and Diana Krall.

Terra Blues
🄢 A, B, C,D, E, F, Q: W 4th St/ Washington Square; 6: Bleecker St

149 Bleecker St, between Thompson and LaGuardia
☎ 1 212 777-7776
Comfortable and friendly, down home blues saloon on the 2nd floor.

Village Vanguard
🄢 1, 2, 3: 14th St 178 7th Ave South at 11th St
☎ 1 212 255-4037
Pulled in John Coltrane, Thelonius Monk and Charles Mingus in their heyday and it's still cookin'.

DANCELAND

New York's dance clubs are a special breed. Many have doormen who limit entry to those with the "right" look. If you can get past the velvet ropes, you'll usually find steep admission fees, jaw-droppingly expensive drinks, no smoking and often, no real dance floor. Still, these places are packed every night by enthusiastic crowds.

APT
🄢 A, C, E, 1, 2, 3: 14th St 419 W 31st St at 9th Ave
☎ 1 212 414-4245
Legendary lounge in the heart of the trendy Meatpacking District, this is a place to dance, drink, see and be seen.

The Hook
🄢 F, G: Carroll St and 12 min. walk
bus B61 to Van Brunt and Commerce Sts 18 Commerce St at Columbia St, Brooklyn
☎ 1 718 797-3007
Alternative rock concerts in a desolate industrial district of Red Hook; fantastic sound system and huge interior space. Reasonable prices, trendy.

Marquee
🄢 C, E: 23rd St 289 10th Ave between 26th St and 27th St
☎ 1 646 473-0202
A stylish Chelsea space attracting youngish celebrities and those who hope to see them.

Opera
🄢 C, E: 50th St 268 W 47th St between Broadway and 8th Ave
☎ 1 212 398-3800
Known for its VIP lounge and outdoor terrace. From R&B and reggae to classic and hip-hop.

Webster Hall
🄢 N, R, 4, 5, 6: 14th St/Union Square 125 E 11th St
☎ 1 212 353-1600
Five floors, each with a distinctive style of music. Trapeze artists and occasional live music.

cityFacts

Accommodation

It's best to make hotel reservations well in advance of your arrival. If, for some reason, you find yourself in Manhattan with nowhere to stay, call Accommodations Plus International at 1 800-733-ROOM. They will try to help you book a room and won't charge you a commission for their service.

Airports

Three major airports serve the New York City area:

John F. Kennedy (JFK) International Airport, Queens
☎ 1 718 244-4444

Newark Liberty International Airport (EWR), New Jersey
☎ 1 973 961-6000

LaGuardia Airport (LAG), Queens
☎ 1 718 533-3400

One of the most disconcerting aspects of your trip to New York might well be figuring out how to get from the airport to your hotel. After you've claimed your luggage and made it through customs, you'll see signs everywhere announcing the various modes of transportation to New York City. JFK and Newark International airports are huge complexes, and even New Yorkers lose their way if they're not careful.

One of the simplest ways to and from the local airports is by yellow cab. Rates for the ride from JFK have been standardized: $45 to any destination in Manhattan. Taxis from Newark Liberty International Airport usually cost $40–55. A cab from LaGuardia Airport will run $25–$29, depending on traffic conditions. None of these fares include tolls (about $4), or a tip.

The next best bet is by bus. Relatively cheap (about $13–15 from any of the airports), they will take you to midtown Manhattan, where you can get a taxi to your hotel. The following companies serve the airports:

Super Shuttle (JFK, LAG and EWR)
☎ 1 800 258-3826 (toll free) or 1 212 209-7000

New York Airport Service (JFK and LAG)
☎ 1 212 875-8200

Olympia Trails Airport Express (EWR)
☎ 1 877 894-9155 (toll free) or 1 908 354-3330

To return to the airport, the same bus companies take passengers from midtown (southeast corner of Park Ave and 42nd St) to the three major airports. Of course, you can always catch a taxi, though the same standardized fare does not apply for the return trip to JFK. Expect to pay about $40–45 to JFK and Newark Liberty International and $30 to LaGuardia Airport, without tip and tolls.

Avoid road traffic by using the AirTrain light-rail system. Newark AirTrain connects with Amtrak and NJ TRANSIT trains at the Newark Liberty International Airport station; the JFK AirTrain connects to the subway, the Long Island Rail Road trains and to local buses. It costs less than $10 to go between Manhattan and JFK by AirTrain and subway.

Business Hours

The city never sleeps—you can get a meal, work out, buy toothpaste, cigarettes, beer or a bouquet of flowers at 3am if you like. Shops generally open Monday to Saturday 10am to 6pm. Most stores are open Sunday as well, though it's best to call ahead and check. The large department stores often remain open well into the evening (9 or 10pm) and many also open on Sunday. Many of the large electronics and camera stores are owned by Orthodox Jews, and are closed late Friday and all day Saturday to observe the Sabbath.

Most banks are open Monday to Saturday 9am–3 or 3.30pm. Some remain open until 6pm daily and Commerce Bank is also open on Sundays.

Climate

The best seasons for visiting New York are spring and autumn. In summer, June, July and August, temperatures average 25–28°C (77–82°F) but may reach extremes of 39°C (102°F)! The coldest winter months are January and February, with temperatures averaging around 0°C (32°F). (Americans still measure temperatures in Fahrenheit.)

Consulates

British citizens requiring consular assistance can get in touch with their Consul:

845 3rd Avenue (between 51st St and 52nd St)
☎ 1 212 745-0200, fax 1 212 745-3062

The British Embassy in Washington, D.C. handles more serious matters:

3100 Massachusetts Ave, NW
☎ 1 202 588-7800

Australian Consulate General:

150 E 42nd St, 34th floor (near Lexington Ave)
☎ 1 212 315-6500, fax 1 212 351-6501

Canadian Consulate General:

1251 Ave of the Americas
☎ 1 212 596-1628, fax 1 212 596-1790
Canadian citizens needing emergency help can call collect:
☎ 1 613 996-8885 or communicate via TTY by dialing 1 800 394-3472 or 1 613 944-1310

Customs and Entry Formalities

All international visitors, regardless of their country of origin, must present a passport or secure document when entering the US by air. Children must have their own passports. Check with your local US consulate, embassy or the Department of State Web site (www.travel.state.gov) before your trip to see what is required for entry into the US. Passports issued by Visa Waiver Program countries must be e-Passports, which include an integrated computer chip. If you are travelling on the Visa Waiver Program you must register online, at least 72 hours before departure, on:

https://esta.cbp.dhs.gov

Tourists are not allowed to bring certain types of animal and agricultural products into the country, and carrying drugs will get you into a lot of trouble. Check the US Customs and Border Protection (CBP) Web site for guidelines and information on customs inspections (www.cbp.gov).

Rules and regulations for flights leaving the US change extremely frequently; the best way to be up-to-date is by looking at the Transportation Security Administration's Web site (www.tsa.gov/travelers/).

Disabled Visitors

Public buildings constructed since 1987 are required to be accessible to the disabled; many older buildings have added ramps, automatic doors or other modified entrances. City buses are equipped with wheelchair lifts located at the front or middle of the vehicle; you may need to ask the driver to lower the lift. If you wish to enter a subway station but are unable to go through the turnstiles, a clerk can open a special gate. However, many subway stations lack disabled access to the trains themselves. If you can't easily navigate stairs, ask the booth attendant whether an elevator is available and working before you pay the non-refundable fare.

Driving

Driving in the traffic-clogged streets of New York is to be avoided at all costs (and parking is nearly impossible), but if you're interested in exploring outside the city, a car is indeed useful. The toll-free numbers of the major rental agencies are listed below. When you ask for prices, make sure they quote you the all-inclusive fee, complete with taxes and insurance charges.

Avis: ☎ (800) 331-1212
Budget: ☎ (800) 527-0700
Hertz: ☎ (800) 654-3131

Electric Current

The standard electrical current in the US is 110 volt 60-cycle AC. Travellers with laptops, alarm clocks, hair-dryers, rechargeable batteries or mobile phones should invest in a transformer and an adapter plug before leaving home. Otherwise, any electronics store is bound to have what you need.

Emergencies

To call an ambulance, the police or the fire department, dial 911 from any phone. The call is free and the service is available 24 hours a day.

BRINGING IT ALL BACK HOME

Spend time shopping and inevitably you'll spot a bargain price on a large or fragile item. But how are you going to get it home? At the larger stores and high-end boutiques, sales assistants can advise you about overseas shipping policies and some will ship your purchases for you. Make sure you understand what to do if the item arrives damaged—or, if doesn't arrive at all.

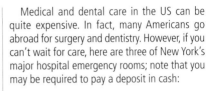

Medical and dental care in the US can be quite expensive. In fact, many Americans go abroad for surgery and dentistry. However, if you can't wait for care, here are three of New York's major hospital emergency rooms; note that you may be required to pay a deposit in cash:

St Vincent's Hospital
170 W 12th St at 7th Ave
☎ 1 212 604-7000

Roosevelt Hospital
1000 10th Ave at 59th St
☎ 1 212 523-4000

NYU Medical Center
550 1st Ave at 33rd St
☎ 1 212 263-7300

For urgent dental treatment, you can call:
Isaac Datikashvili, DMD
77 E 12th Street (at 4th Ave)
☎ 1 212 486-9458 or 1 646 301-7758
Open 24 hours, 7 days a week

Lost Property

If you lose anything on a bus or in the subway, call 1 212 712 4500. Call 311 for property lost in taxis.

Media

To learn what's going on in the city and throughout the world, the best newspaper in town is *The New York Times*. For information on show times, events, concerts, galleries and museum exhibitions, your best bets are *Time Out New York* and *New York Magazine*. News is broadcast, almost to excess, on many television channels. For international news, try CNN and for local reports, tune in to NY1, which provides news about the city 24 hours a day. Most newsstands and magazine stores stock newspapers and magazines from round the world.

Money Matters
The US dollar ($) is divided into 100 cents (¢). Coins are 1¢ (penny), 5¢ (nickel), 10¢ (dime) and 25¢ (quarter), with 50¢ (half-dollar) and $1 coins encountered infrequently. Banknotes in general circulation are $1, $5, $10, $20, $50 and $100. You would do well to depend on travellers cheques and a credit card, with a little cash for small expenditures. When you cash travellers cheques, $20 bills are the handiest: a rash of counterfeiting has made many merchants wary of $50 and $100 notes. It's a good idea to keep some change in your pockets, in case you want to buy a postage stamp or make a phone call.

The larger banks in the midtown area will exchange foreign currency, as will the exchange counters at the three major airports. The best way to exchange currency is to use your debit or credit card to withdraw money from Automated Teller Machines (ATMs—cash distributors); the bank rates are nearly always better than those offered at the exchange counters. ATMs can be found nearly everywhere and operate 24 hours a day.

Pharmacies
For medicines or toiletries, try one of these pharmacies, open 24 hrs:

Walgreen's: 145 4th Ave at 14th St (and numerous other locations)
☎ 1 212 677-0054

Duane Reade: 4 Times Square near Broadway (and other locations)
☎ 1 646 366-8047

CVS: 400 W 59th St at Columbus Ave
☎ 1 212 245-0617

Post Offices

Hours vary, but post offices are generally open Mon–Sat 8am– 6pm. The biggest—and busiest—post office is located across from Penn Station at 421 8th Ave, between 31st and 33rd Sts. It's open seven days a week, 24 hours a day. Stamps are also sold at many pharmacies and supermarkets.

Public Holidays

Instead of closing down, many stores take advantage of a federal (nation-wide) holiday by having a sale. However, most museums, government offices, post offices and banks will shut their doors on the following holidays:

January 1	New Year's Day
3rd Monday in January	Martin Luther King Day
3rd Monday in February	Presidents Day
Last Monday in May	Memorial Day
July 4	Independence Day
1st Monday in September	Labor Day
2nd Monday in October	Columbus Day
November 11	Veterans' Day
4th Tuesday in November	Thanksgiving
December 25	Christmas Day

Public Transport

New York has one of the best public transport systems in the world, and the only system in the US that operates round the clock. Laminated bus/subway maps are sold in most magazine stores, and free bus and subway maps are available at stations.

For $2, you can travel to just about any section in the five boroughs. A MetroCard (sold at subway stations and in over 4000 stores) allows access to and free transfers from local buses and subways. Two versions are available: pay-per-ride and unlimited ride. With pay-per-ride, you buy as many rides as you want from $2 to $81. Put $7 or more on your card and receive a 15 percent bonus. For example, a $20 purchase gives you $23 on your card. Unlimited ride cards, which are valid for a specified period (one day, seven days, 30 days), are easier to understand and use. However, Unlimited

Ride MetroCards cannot be used more than once every 18 minutes. That means that if you travel with a companion, you'll each need your own Unlimited Ride card.

Buses. The Manhattan buses run up or down the avenues (with the exception of Park Ave above 39th St) and cross-town along the major two-way streets. Bus stops are indicated by small red, white and blue signs. In many cases, there are bus shelters near the signs. Either check your map or have a look at the rectangular box on the signpost to find out which route the bus follows. When you board the bus, insert your MetroCard into the steel receptacle near the driver. If you want to travel across town and then up- or downtown (or vice-versa), don't worry; transfers are automatically calculated on your card. To alight, press anywhere on one of the thin rubber strands running the length of the interior as you near your stop and the bus will pull over.

Subway. The subway operates 24 hours a day, and you pay the fare with a MetroCard. You may purchase one inside the station at the booth (ask for a free map, too) or from a vending machine (they accept cash, credit and debit cards). Swipe your MetroCard at the turnstile and walk through. Always stand well clear of the edge of the platform (don't fall!), try to stick with the crowds after dark, and avoid empty subway cars; if no one is sitting in a particular car, there is usually a good reason. Caution: subway maintenance and repair work is usually scheduled for weekends; during those periods, many trains are cancelled or re-routed. Before you enter a subway station on a weekend, check the posted signs or consult the booth attendant to ensure that the train is running as scheduled. Or check www.mta.info for Service Advisories.

Ferries. New York has both public and private ferry services. Most of the private services go to New Jersey and are strictly for commuters. The publicly operated ferry from Manhattan to Staten Island is free and provides outstanding views of the Harbour and the Statue of Liberty.

Taxis. Private transportation is more expensive than public, but sometimes (especially late at night or when you are laden with shopping bags) it is a wiser option.

Drivers of yellow taxi cabs are required by law to take you to any destination in the five boroughs and are required to assist disabled passengers.

If the middle small box on the roof of the taxi is illuminated, the cab is available for hire. You can descend on the right or the left side of the street.

The cost for a taxi ride is $2.50 upon entry and for the first 1/5 mile, 40 cents for each additional 1/5 mile or for every minute if you're stuck in traffic. All rides between 8pm and 6am carry a 50-cent surcharge, and rides Monday to Friday between 4 and 8 pm carry a $1 surcharge. All tolls are the passenger's responsibility. Your driver will expect a minimum 15% tip.

Water Taxis. These bright yellow boats serve well-heeled commuters and connect points in Manhattan, Brooklyn and a sand-covered party wharf in Queens (open only in summer) called Water Taxi Beach. They also offer tours, cruises and hop on and off service. The fare, which varies with the trip and route, ranges from $3.00 to $10; a 2-day hop on and off ticket is $25 for adults, $15 for kids. There is also a free Water Taxi shuttle that goes from Pier 11 on Wall Street to the IKEA store in Red Hook, Brooklyn.

Safety

It's best to abide by a few rules of thumb during your visit. Be careful, don't flaunt your jewellery, cash and credit cards, don't leave your belongings unattended and avoid long, empty city blocks after dark. It's a good idea to leave anything irreplacable at home, stash valuables in the hotel safe, use travellers cheques and credit cards when and where you can, and carry your camera, cell phone, iPod or laptop discreetly . In other words, use your common sense, act as you would in any large city and you should be fine.

It may happen that a panhandler will approach you; it's probably best just to ignore him. If you opt to give money, do so and move on quickly.

Don't be afraid of New York: whatever scary stories you may have read, the fact is that New York is the safest big city in the US. And keep in mind that some 1.5 million people live, work, play, eat, sleep and raise their children on the island of Manhattan.

Taxes

There is an 8.375% sales tax on many goods (including electronics and jewellery) and personal services (beauty salons, massages, etc.). For clothing and footwear, the rate drops to 4.375%. There is also a tax of about 14% on hotel rooms.

Telephones

To a great extent, mobile phones have replaced the coin-operated public telephone booths that once stood on nearly every street corner, but they are still available in most hotels, train and bus stations and large department stores. In subway stations, a yellow handpiece indicates that the phone can be used to place international calls.

A quarter (25¢) will get you three minutes locally. Each additional minute requires an extra deposit. Rather than filling your pockets with coins, you can use a prepaid phone card, available at most news stands and delis.

If you're dialling within Manhattan, you must first dial 1 plus the area code, either 212, 646 or 917. To call Brooklyn, Queens, the Bronx or Staten Island from Manhattan, dial 1 and the area code (718, 347 or 917) then the 7-digit number. When you use a public phone, a recorded voice will tell you how much to deposit. Always have change or a phone card handy. To obtain an address, dial 411 for directory assistance.

For long distance calls in the US, dial 1, then the area code, then the 7-digit number. To call the UK from anywhere in the US, dial 011 44, the area code and the local number.

To speak with an international operator, dial 00. To speak to a local operator (if you're having trouble completing a call), dial 0. And always remember, for an emergency just dial 911. For information and help with city matters, call 311.

Time

The 24-hour clock is only used in the US by the military services. Otherwise, the US sticks to am and pm. New York is on Eastern Standard Time, GMT −5 (with daylight saving time from April to October, GMT −4).

Tipping

While tipping isn't mandatory, it would be extremely unorthodox to forego it, especially at a bar or restaurant—waiters and bartenders count on tips to earn a decent wage. The customary tipping rate is 15–20%. An easy way to figure out the proper tip for a meal is to double the tax and, if you're feeling generous, add a dollar or two. Cloakroom attendants will expect $1 per coat, hotel maids $1 a day and porters $2. Hairdressers, manicurists and taxi drivers should receive 15–20%.

Toilets
Unfortunately, public toilets are something of a rarity in New York. You can find them in parks and public buildings such as Penn Station and Grand Central Terminal, but they are not always clean and tend to attract the homeless. Best to use the "restrooms", as the Americans call them, in museums, hotels, theatres, department stores, bookstores, fast food places and coffeehouses.

Only patrons are allowed to use the restrooms in restaurants, but in fast food places and coffeehouses you can gain access to the WC simply by buying a cup of coffee.

Tourist Information
The city's official tourist offices provide extensive information on events, tours, restaurants, museums, sightseeing, shopping, children's activities and transport. Stop by to pick up maps and brochures:

NYC&Co
810 7th Ave at 53rd St
☎ 1 212 484-1200
Daily 8am–8pm

Federal Hall Information Center
26 Wall Street (inside Federal Hall)
Mon–Fri 9am–5pm

Chinatown Visitor Center
Kiosk at Canal and Baxter Streets
Daily 10am–6pm

NYC Heritage Tourism Center
Kiosk at Broadway and Park Row (next to City Hall Park)
Mon–Fri 9am–6pm, Sat and Sun 10am–5pm

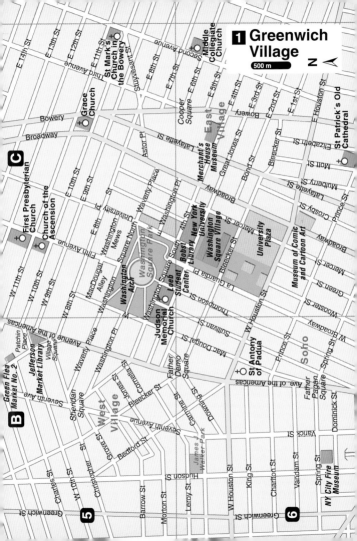

1 Greenwich Village

500 m

N

C

St Mark's Church in the Bowery
Middle Collegiate Church
Second Avenue
E 13th St
E 12th St
E 11th St
E 10th St
E 9th St
E 8th St
E 7th St
E 6th St
E 5th St
E 4th St
E 3rd St
E 2nd St
E 1st St
E Houston St
Third Avenue
Stuyvesant St
Cooper Square
Astor Pl
Lafayette St
Grace Church
Bowery
Broadway
Merchant's House Museum
East Village
St Patrick's Old Cathedral
Elizabeth St
Mott St
Mulberry St
Lafayette St
Crosby St
Bond St
Bleecker St
Great Jones St

First Presbyterian Church
Church of the Ascension
Fifth Avenue
W 11th St
W 10th St
W 9th St
W 8th St
University Place
University Place
Washington Mews
Washington Square North
Waverly Place
New York University
Bobst Library
Washington Square Village
University Plaza
Museum of Comic and Cartoon Art
Mercer St
Greene St
Wooster St
Broadway
Crosby St

Washington Square Park
Washington Arch
Washington Square South
Loeb Student Center
Judson Memorial Church
MacDougal Alley
Washington Pl
Thompson St
La Guardia Pl
Mercer St
Bleecker St
W Houston St
St Antony of Padua
Ave of the Americas

B
Green Flea Market No. 2
Patchin Place
Jefferson Market Library
Village Square
Waverly Place
Avenue of the Americas
Father Demo Square
Sixth Avenue
MacDougal St
Sullivan St
Thompson St
Prince St
Soho
Father Pagan Square
Spring St
W Broadway

West Village
Seventh Avenue
Sheridan Square
Grove St
W 10th St
Christopher St
Bleecker St
Bedford St
Barrow St
Morton St
Leroy St
Carmine St
Commerce St
Jones St
Cornelia St
Downing St
James J Walker Park
Hudson St
W Houston St
King St
Charlton St
Vandam St
Varick St
Dominick St
NY City Fire Museum
Greenwich St

Charles St
W 10th St
Greenwich St

5

6

B

C

2

Pier 83

Intrepid Sea-Air-Space Museum

Dewitt Clinton Park

Lincoln Tunnel

Greyhound Bus Lines

Theater District

J. K. Javits Exhibition and Convention Center of N. Y.

3

Port Authority Bus Terminal

New York Times

Eleventh Avenue

Tenth Avenue

Ninth Avenue

Eighth Avenue

Seventh Avenue

49th

48th St

47th St

46th St

45th

44th

43rd

42nd

41st

40th

39th

38th

37th St

36th

35th St

34th St

33rd St

W 49th St

W 48th St

W 44th St

W 43rd St

W 42nd St

W 41st St

W 40th St

39th St

38th St

37th St

36th St

35th St

Tenth Avenue

Eleventh Avenue

Ninth Avenue

Eighth Avenue

5th St

50th

W 32nd St

30th St

29th St

31st St

27th St

W 27th St

W 26th St

W 25th St

24th St

Chelsea Park

Penn Station and Madison Square Garden

Pennsylvania Station

Macy's

34th St

Avenue of the Americas

Empire State Bldg.

W 32nd St

30th St

29th St

28th St

26th St

25th St

Broadway

4

2 Midtown Manhattan

N

200 m

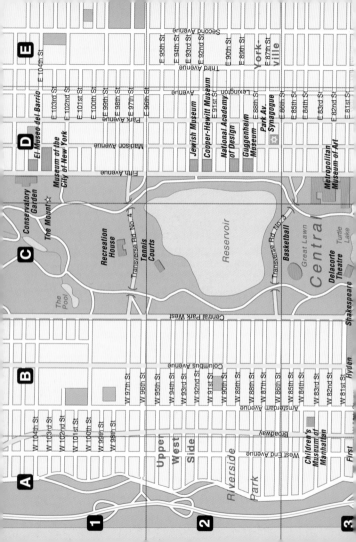

250 m

N

Second Avenue
Third Avenue
Lexington Avenue
Park Avenue
Madison Avenue
Fifth Avenue
Central Park West
Columbus Avenue
Broadway
West End Avenue
Eighth Avenue
Seventh Avenue
Sixth Avenue
Central Park South
Central Park South

Temple Shaaray Tefila
Upper East Side
E 77th St
E 75th St
E 71st St
Lenox Hill Hospital
Harkness House
Whitney Museum of American Art
E 78th St
E 76th St
E 74th St
E 73rd St
E 72nd St
E 70th St
E 69th St
E 67th St
E 65th St
E 64th St
E 62nd St
E 61st St
E 60th St
E 59th St
E 58th St
E 57th St

St James Church
Knoedler & Co.
Asia Society Gallery
St V. Ferrer Church
Frick Collection
Templ Emanu-El
Children's Zoo
Zoo
Synagogue
Grand Army Plaza
Barney's
Plaza Hotel
Trump Tower
Park Ave Citibank
Plaza
G. M. Corp.

Central Park
The Glade
Cedar Hill
Conservatory Pond
The Ramble
The Lake
Belvedere Castle
Boat House
Bethesda Fountain
Cherry Hill
Strawberry Fields
Bowling Greens
The Mall
Sheep Meadow
Transverse Rd. No. 1
Carousel
Skating rink
Bird Sanctuary
The Pond
Heckscher Playground

Museum of Modern Art
Museum of Arts & Design
Olympic Towers
Fifth Avenue

Tourist Info.

Tavern on the Green
Holy Trinity Lutheran Church
Avery Fisher Hall
Museum for Performing Arts
Lincoln Center
Metropolitan Opera House
N.Y. State Theater
Fordham University
St Paul the Apostle
Coliseum
Columbus Circle

American Museum of Natural History
N.Y. Historical Society
Sherman Square

W 78th St
W 77th St
W 76th St
W 75th St
W 74th St
W 73rd St
W 72nd St
W 71st St
W 70th St
W 69th St
W 68th St
W 67th St
W 66th St
W 65th St
W 64th St
W 63rd St
W 62nd St
W 61st St
W 60th St
W 59th St
W 58th St

W 57th St
W 56th St
W 55th St
W 54th St
W 53rd St

Broadway

4

5

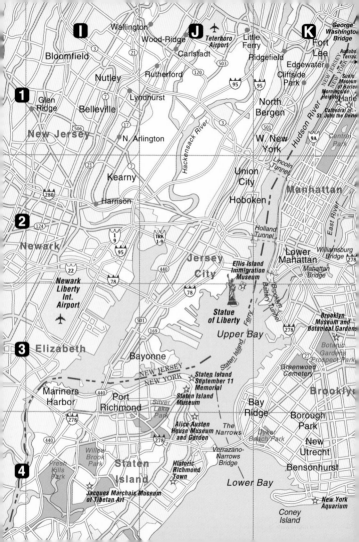

4 New York City

2.5 km

General Editor: Barbara Ender
Editor: Petronella Greenhalgh
Features and Research: Anne Samachson
Layout: Luc Malherbe, Matias Jolliet
Maps: Elsner & Schichor, JPM Publications, MTA Metropolitan Transportation Authority
Photo credits: hemis.fr/Pérousse p. 4; /Renaut pp. 6 (left), 70;
/Maisant: pp. 6 (centre) 60; /Rieger pp. 7, 57, 98; /Giraudou p. 8 (centre).
Anne Samachson pp. 7 (right), 15, 16, 31, 32, 41, 45, 47, 51, 64, 69, 72, 76, 77,
  80, 81, 83, 84, 85, 86, 88, 89, 95.
Bildagentur Huber/Pignatelli p. 8; /Gräfenhain p. 43.
istockphoto.com/AF Kazmierski p. 11; /J Pauls p. 13; /M Bergheiser p. 17;
/F van den Bergh p. 18; /C Steer pp. 21, 93; /L Merz: p. 22; /L Vorfeld p. 25;/J Cicak: p. 87;
/J Chapman p. 78; /lillisphotography p. 85 (bottom); /Terraxplorer p. 90; /E Serrabassa p. 94.
fotolia/Brosig p. 12. Jean Mohr p. 26. Jean-Paul Minder: pp. 35, 54, 55, 104.
Jeff Greenberg/NYC&Company p. 48.
Thanks to Susan Cagle for permission to use her photo p. 17